THE ESSENTIAL TRUDEAU

Pierre Elliott Trudeau

THE
ESSENTIAL
TRUDEAU

Edited by Ron Graham

Excerpts from *Towards a Just Society: The Trudeau Years*, edited by
Thomas S. Axworthy and Pierre Elliott Trudeau, translated into
English by Patricia Claxton. Copyright © for the selection 90562
Canada Ltée and Axiom Strategy Group Inc. 1990. Copyright ©
this edition, Penguin Books Canada Limited 1990. Reprinted by
permission of Penguin Books Canada Limited.

Excerpts from *Approaches to Politics* by Pierre Elliott Trudeau,
translated by I. M. Owen. © Les Éditions du Jour Inc. 1970.
Translation © Oxford University Press (Canadian Branch) 1970.
Reprinted by permission of Oxford University Press Canada.

Excerpts from *The Asbestos Strike* edited by Pierre Elliott Trudeau,
translated by James Boake. Translation © James Lewis & Samuel
(James Lorimer & Co. Ltd.) 1974. Reprinted by permission.

Canadian Cataloguing in Publication Data

Trudeau, Pierre Elliott, 1919-
The essential Trudeau

ISBN 0-7710-8591-5

1. Canada – Politics and government – 1935- .
2. Trudeau, Pierre Elliott, 1919- – Political and social views.
I. Graham, Ron, 1948- . II. Title.

FC600.T782 1998   971.064   C98-931082-5
F1034.2.T78 1998

We acknowledge the financial support of the Government of
Canada through the Book Publishing Industry Development
Program for our publishing activities. We further acknowledge the
support of the Canada Council for the Arts and the Ontario Arts
Council for our publishing program.

Typeset in Minion by M&S, Toronto

Printed and bound in Canada

McClelland & Stewart, Inc.
The Canadian Publishers
481 University Avenue
Toronto, Ontario
M5G 2E9

1 2 3 4 5 6   03 02 01 00 99 98

CONTENTS

INTRODUCTION

The person who most doubted whether the world needed another book by Pierre Trudeau was Pierre Trudeau. He certainly didn't relish the work involved or crave more public attention. Unlike many retired leaders, he isn't eager to proffer his opinions about current events, which he follows only sporadically and from a distance, nor is he interested in spending the remainder of his years sniping at his successors and harking back to better days. Even more unusual, he is neither obsessed by his place in history nor convinced that people care what he thinks. He's genuinely surprised by the crowds who still turn out to see him, the invitations he still gets to speak (but never accepts), and the media coverage he still garners without seeking it. Far from thinking himself indispensable to the survival and well-being of the nation, he has counted on new people and new generations to pick up his struggle for a just and united Canada.

There have been a few notable exceptions, of course, more notable for being few. As a concerned citizen who knows something about constitutional reform, he felt compelled to speak out against the

Meech Lake and Charlottetown accords. He thought they would be bad for the country, for the many reasons he enumerated at the time, and nothing has persuaded him that Canada would be in better shape, not worse, had either accord succeeded. In several instances he was pressed by friends and former colleagues to participate in written and televised accounts of their time in government. He only acquiesced after overcoming a strong reluctance. Most recently, at the urging of his publisher, he allowed his dear friend the late Gérard Pelletier to assemble an extensive selection of his writings, most of which had been scattered in small journals and commentary pages over more than fifty years. (This was published as *Against the Current* in 1996.)

And there, perhaps, he might have withdrawn into what Pascal called "le silence éternal de ces espaces infinis," content to commend his actions and beliefs to the judgement of God and history – except for two considerations. The first was the degree to which his ideas have remained the objects of misinterpretation and misrepresentation. That is understandable, maybe even forgivable, from partisan opponents, whether the anti-liberals in Ottawa or the anti-federalists in Quebec. It is much less understandable or forgivable from academics, journalists, and other commentators who should know better. Secondly, and more passing strange, was the number of times he has been asked the same fundamental questions with respect to the same fundamental issues: Isn't there a positive side to nationalism? What's so bad about recognizing Quebec as a distinct society? Aren't there collective rights as well as individual rights? Isn't it proper, for the sake of personal freedom or balanced budgets, to reduce the role of government in general and the central government in particular? And so on.

Not surprisingly, if he responds at all, he responds with the same fundamental answers. Or perhaps that is surprising. Politicians are not expected to hold consistent views – for weeks, let alone decades – rooted in a set of basic ideas. (When Harold Macmillan was asked to come up with a collective phrase for politicians equivalent to a herd of cows or gaggle of geese, he immediately suggested "a lack of principles.") In Trudeau's case, however, he had devoted a prolonged period of his youth to studying the great questions of political philosophy with the express desire to arrive at propositions that could reasonably be accepted as true and, therefore, constant. His critics interpreted his constancy as dogmatism, inflexibility, and sheer pigheadedness. His admirers more charitably called it adherence to principles. Either way, amid the pandemonium of power and the quiet of retirement, he found little cause to disown what he had written ten, twenty, thirty, even forty years earlier about personal liberty, ethnic nationalism, democracy, and federalism.

That's not to suggest that he never adapted his theories to evolving circumstances or practical politics. The very importance he placed on the liberal concept of checks and balances – what he usually called counterweights – compelled him to avoid ideological rigidity. At times, in other words, he found it not only acceptable but desirable to shift tactics in order to protect individual freedom, the weaker segments of society, and the federal system from undue concentrations of power. Thus, what might have looked like a contradiction of his principles was often their reaffirmation. Not always, of course. There were times when the realities of power and politics made contradictions unavoidable. But Trudeau was an exception among long-lasting political leaders for his intellectual consistency. Ideas always matter in politics, but rarely in Canadian history have they mattered more than during his prime-ministership.

Yet, despite what's been termed an industry of books, articles, and documentaries about the Trudeau years, a whole series of myths, errors, and outright lies has taken a stubborn hold. It's peculiar, and probably revealing, that those who have been most vocal in accusing him of recycling old material just happen to be those who have been most consistent in misinterpreting and misunderstanding him.

For counterbalancing the strong provinces with a strong federal government, he was branded a centralist – even though he argued in favour of strengthening the provinces in the 1950s and gave them unprecedented resources in the 1970s. For counterbalancing the strong corporations with a strong state, he was branded a socialist – even though he opposed the nationalization of Quebec's hydro companies in the 1960s and entrenched the rights and freedoms of individuals in the 1980s. His efforts to strengthen Canada vis-à-vis the United States were confused with the ethnic nationalism he so adamantly opposed in both English-speaking Canada and French-speaking Quebec. His lifelong devotion to multiculturalism as a key to social tolerance, democratic pluralism, and individual fulfilment was twisted to appear like a ploy to undermine the two-nations theory of Confederation, a ruse to capture the immigrant vote, a sop to Western Canada's pioneer communities, and an argument for collective rights.

The pervasiveness of such deliberate or ignorant distortions ultimately persuaded him of the usefulness of yet another effort at restating and explaining his basic principles. It's like the old priest who, when asked why he stood up in his pulpit Sunday after Sunday and simply recited the Ten Commandments over and over again, replied, "I'll keep repeating them until you get them right."

But perhaps there was a better – or at least novel – way to get his message over the heads of these jaded, self-serving élites directly to the people, as he had tried to do in power. Perhaps his essays were too academic and lengthy. Perhaps his interventions were too legalistic and detailed. So the notion gradually emerged – inspired, however modestly, by Pascal's *Pensées* and the *Analects* of Confucius – to strip away the learned references and contemporary allusions in his writings and speeches in order to reveal the very core of his political and social thought. The next step was to rearrange the resulting fragments into thematic sections that had a logical order building towards a comprehensive vision. And, finally, after a great deal of prodding, Trudeau agreed to add a series of informal commentaries – which have been italicized to distinguish them from the text – as a way to connect the theory to his practice of politics.

My role as editor was to go through Trudeau's writings and speeches, extract the essence from them, and order them according to theme, logic, and number. In almost every case, they have been left as they appeared in the original or in an authorized translation. But, just as Trudeau had been given that rarest of things, a second chance as a politician, so he was given a second chance as a writer. He took advantage of it to make some minor modifications for the sake of clarity, to repair a faulty construction or two, and to update certain usages. In several places he has changed tenses from present to past in recognition of a change of circumstances. And, throughout, as he explains more fully at the start of Section XIV, he has italicized *nation, national, nationalism, nationalist, nationality,* and so forth, whenever he means them in the ethnic or sociological sense, as a way of clearly differentiating them from the same words used (without italics) in the political or civic sense. All significant alterations have been indicated in the source notes, along with the sources and dates.

This book is intended to be neither an apology for his life nor a souvenir item. Its purpose is to serve, by its accessibility and compactness, as a pocket guide to the miles of Trudeau papers in the National Archives and a clear, authoritative summation of what Pierre Trudeau has stood for, what he wanted to accomplish in office, and why. And that's the sense in which it is essential.

RON GRAHAM

THE ESSENTIAL TRUDEAU

I

THE DOMAIN OF POLITICS

1

We are going to be governed whether we like it or not; it is up to us to see to it that we are governed no worse than is absolutely unavoidable. We must therefore concern ourselves with politics, as Pascal said, to mitigate as far as possible the damage done by the madness of our rulers.

2

The first thing to ask of history is that it should point out to us the paths of liberty. The great lesson to draw from revolutions is not that they devour humanity but rather that tyranny never fails to generate them.

3

The price of liberty, say the English, is eternal vigilance. But to be vigilant one must be aware of one's rights. It is important, then, to know what our freedom is founded on, and how far the state has authority to restrict it. In other words, strict limits must be placed on the right of one person to rule another. This is indeed the domain of politics.

THE GIFT OF LIBERTY

I used to take religion very literally. If God was God and Christ was his son, then certain things followed and you had to be quite strict in your beliefs and morals. But, as I began studying philosophy and theology, I had to confront the fundamental question of liberty. If God knows what is going to happen, does that mean you are programmed, predestined? Then I began to read Thomas Aquinas, who makes a distinction between the morals of a slave and the morals of a prince. A slave obeys the commandments of the Church because he has to, whereas a prince is the master of his soul and decides by himself what to obey. So, as a free man, I began to reinterpret some of the dogmas and ethics. I kept talking about freedom of choice and about conscience as the ultimate recourse for every human being. As a result, I was often thought more of a Protestant than a Catholic.

Even when I was a student, a lot of my foolishness and a lot of my writings were about man's freedom. I liked the temperament of Cyrano de Bergerac, the idea of a man who does his own thing, who has his own ideals, and who fights anybody who tries to get in his way. Let's not follow conventions, fashions, or accepted opinions. Let's be ourselves and seek new truths for ourselves. Like Cyrano, maybe we won't climb very high, but at least we'll climb alone, without owing anybody anything. And even when I was prime minister, I didn't like to ask for favours due my rank. I'd be embarrassed when they made me jump a queue to get into a ball game or something. I'd look the other way.

4

In the normal course of life we are subject to many constraints, and we do not hesitate to impose others on ourselves if need be; we are able to accept them as mechanisms indispensable to our life, as the framework of our liberty – for liberty is not without form. And the price of our liberty may be a momentary surrender of one particular freedom. This is undoubtedly the highest price we can pay for liberty, next to giving our life itself. But liberty is worth this sacrifice. With the love which gives it life, liberty remains the most difficult conquest for humanity. Liberty can thrive only if consciously nurtured; liberty is never won for all time; liberty never sleeps.

5

I have never been able to accept any discipline except that which I imposed upon myself – and there was a time when I used to impose it often. For, in the art of living, as in that of loving, or of governing – it is all the same – I found it unacceptable that others should claim to know better than I what was good for me. Consequently, I found tyranny completely intolerable.

6

In Canada, and this includes Quebec, we have never known tyranny except in its figurative forms, for example, the tyranny of public opinion. I am, however, far from considering that particular form the least terrible. For public opinion seeks to impose its domination over everything. Its aim is to reduce all action, all thought, and all feeling to a common denominator. It forbids independence and kills inventiveness; condemns those who ignore it and banishes those who oppose it.

At certain times, on certain subjects, the government is either behind the people or in step with the people. But I believe a government should also try to be slightly ahead of the people. It must indicate the directions it thinks the society should follow for its future well-being. That's what you might call leadership. However, you can't be too far ahead of the people, too isolated, too dictatorial, or else the people will cease following. You can't lead a people like you can lead a horse.

7

The liberal philosophy sets the highest value on the freedom of the individual, by which we mean the total individual, the individual as a member of a society to which he is inextricably bound by his way of life, and by community of interest and culture. For a liberal, the individual represents an absolute personal value; the human person has a transcending social significance. Concern for the human person is thus at its most intense within the liberal mind. The tolerance of a liberal is exemplary. It forbids any action, or attitude, or omission, that might tend to jeopardize the rights of other individuals.

I was influenced here by my reading of Jacques Maritain and the so-called personalists. Personalism essentially said that the individual, not the state, must be supreme, with basic rights and freedoms, because the individual is the only moral entity, the only one who has significance. But, granted that, we should view the individual as a person involved in society and with responsibilities to it. In other words, sovereign individuals can get together to co-insure each other against the accidents and hazards of living in society. This co-insurance is exercised through the welfare state, by helping those who can't help themselves. I found personalism a good way to distinguish my thinking from the self-centred individualism of laissez-faire liberalism (or modern-day neo-conservatism, for that matter) by bestowing it with a sense of duty to the community in which one is living.

8

The first visible effect of freedom is change. A free man exercises his freedom by altering himself and – inevitably – his surroundings. It follows that no liberal can be other than receptive to change and highly positive and active in his response to it, for change is the very expression of freedom. Clearly, though, a liberal can neither encourage nor accept indiscriminate change by indiscriminate means.

9

Hence a liberal is a person of the left. A liberal can seldom be a partisan of the status quo. He tends to be a reformer – attempting to move society, to modify its institutions, to liberate its citizens. At the same time, the liberal is not an anarchist because he does not believe that a free man can live as a total individual outside society. Nor is the liberal a revolutionary who believes that society must perpetually be scrubbed clean of the tracings of the past, must always begin again from an antiseptic tabula rasa. I like to say that a liberal is on the left, but no farther.

10

There is no absolute truth in politics. The best ideologies, having arisen at specific times to combat given abuses, become the worst if they survive the needs which gave them birth. Throughout history all great reformers were sooner or later betrayed by the excessive fidelity of their disciples. When a reform starts to be universally popular, it is more than likely that it has already become reactionary, and free men must then oppose it.

11

Ideological systems are the true enemies of freedom. On the political front, accepted opinions are not only inhibiting to the mind, they contain the very source of error. When a political ideology is universally accepted by the élite, when the people who "define situations" embrace and venerate it, this means that it is high time free men were fighting it. For political freedom finds its essential strength in a sense of balance and proportion. As soon as any one tendency becomes too strong, it constitutes a menace.

12

Liberty is a free gift – a birthright, which distinguishes people from beasts. To allow human society to develop in order and justice, people agree to some restrictions on their liberty, and obey the authority of the state. In consequence, the game of politics should consist less in wresting liberties from a grudging state than in grudgingly delegating powers to the state.

III

THE BASIS OF AUTHORITY

I had always been taught, at school and university, that authority came from God. But I had to reconcile this authority that came from God with the freedom of the individual that I so strongly believed in. I started from the principle that no one knew what was good for me better than I. So why should I obey my teachers? I should obey them because I am a free man who decides that, in this or that area of knowledge, they know more than I do.

Bringing this to politics, I asked myself why the people obey a prime minister or a king or a dictator, since they themselves know what is important for them better than any authority does. This led me to study liberalism and conclude that democracy is the best vehicle because it permits all individuals together to choose the government. And therefore authority comes from the people. This sat well with my own feeling of independence, while accepting the law and any obligatory customs because I was a social being.

As minister of justice, for example, I had a hard time in cabinet when it came to reforming the laws about divorce, homosexuality, and abortion. There were those who thought, for moral reasons, that I was doing the wrong thing, but I thought it was important to distinguish between a sin and a crime. While I completely respected their belief that this or that was a sin that shouldn't be allowed in the ethics of their religion, we were legislators, not priests or popes. We had to legislate for a pluralist society in which some belonged to other religions or had no religion at all. We had to legislate for a peaceful society that was respectful of people's individual consciences.

Then there were those who had political objections. That's when I said, "The state has no place in the bedrooms of the nation," so long as what's done hurts nobody and is done between consenting adults. I found very early on that the people were generally more ready than the politicians for change, though that wasn't always true, as in the case of the death penalty.

My approach was rooted in the theory of counterweights. At every moment in time, I believe, each conscious servant of the public good must ask himself or herself: In what direction should I be weighing in at this time? Should I be trying to weaken authority or should I be trying to strengthen it? For in a society, if everybody begins to follow a certain fashion, then that fashion becomes a tyranny. Those who don't follow it are looked down upon as being out of fashion and they lose their individuality. And when everybody starts to think or do the same thing, we all lose our freedom.

In that sense I think it's a good thing to challenge authority – not by curse words or dynamite, but by questioning the ideas and values of people who want

*you to follow and obey them. Similarly, any govern-
ment that wants to innovate has to go against the
current of previous times. This is the way individuals,
governments, and countries progress.*

13

The oldest problem of political philosophy, although
it is not the only one, is to justify authority without
destroying the independence of human beings in the
process. How can an individual be reconciled with a
society? The need for privacy with the need to live in
groups? Love of freedom with need for order? The
most useful conclusion philosophy has come to is
that one must keep an equal distance from both
alternatives. Too much authority, or too little, and
that is the end of freedom.

14

The purpose of living in society is that every person
may fulfil himself or herself as far as possible. Authority has no justification except to allow the establish-
ment and development of a system that encourages
such fulfilment in every human being.

15

Human societies differ from beehives in that human
beings are always free to decide what form of authority they will adopt, and who will exercise it. And it
really is human beings who have the responsibility of
taking these decisions – not God, Providence, or

Nature. In the last analysis any given political authority exists only because people consent to obey it. In this sense, what exists is not so much the authority as the obedience.

16

Neither authority nor obedience ought to be taken for granted. If my father, my priest, or my king wants to exert authority over me, if he wants to give me orders, he has to be able to explain, in a way that satisfies my reason, on what grounds he must command and I must obey.

17

When authority in any form bullies a citizen unfairly, all other citizens are guilty; for it is their tacit assent that allows authority to commit the abuse. If they withdrew their consent, authority would collapse.

18

Most people seek only their own comfort and pleasure: when these ends are assured, they ask no more than to conform to a given social order and to obey political masters who work to maintain that order. Few people are aroused by an injustice when they are sure of not being its victim themselves.

19

As long as authority does not pass all bounds of stupidity and incompetence it is sure to hold its position.

20

If the people feel themselves oppressed, appeals to vague and abstract notions of general welfare, established order, and respect for authority will not in practice compel obedience. The people obey because it is easier to do so and because they are accustomed to it; this custom will be broken if the people, feeling themselves oppressed, start thinking about the possibility of suppressing the oppressors.

21

Tyrants always claim that their social order is founded on the common weal, the welfare of the race; but they reserve the right to define this welfare themselves, and their laws require the citizens to act accordingly. Now, to credit one or several leaders with superior knowledge of what particular set of actions is best for everyone is to call into question the very basis of social morality. For the only good action, of real moral value, is a voluntary action, chosen by the enlightened thinking of the person who performs it.

22

No government, no particular régime, has an absolute right to exist. This is not a matter of divine right, natural law, or social contract: a government is an organization whose job is to fulfil the needs of the men and women, grouped in society, who consent to obey it. Consequently the value of a government derives not from the promises it makes, from what it claims to be, or from what it alleges it is defending, but from what it achieves in practice. And it is for each citizen to judge that.

23

If the order is rotten and the authority vicious, the duty of the citizen is to obey his or her conscience in preference to that authority. And if the only sure way of reconstituting a just social order is to stage a revolution *against tyrannical and illegal authority* – well, then, it must be done.

24

When you teach the people to obey authority, you ought to add that it is possible to disobey it with an equally good conscience. If you did so you would find, on the one hand, that the rulers would grow rather more respectful towards the governed; on the other, that the latter would become more sensitive to the notions of liberty and justice.

25

In a society of egoists, clearly, every citizen will want a government that will cater to him personally even at the expense of others: on election day he will therefore pledge his loyalty to a government that will give him, as circumstances require, a bottle of beer, a refrigerator, a church pavement, or a university subsidy.

But a society of egoists quickly becomes a society of slaves; for no one person is capable of overturning an established government. Such a government is not weakened at all when one discontented citizen refuses to obey the authorities, for they simply put him in prison.

To remain free, then, citizens must seek their welfare in a social order that is just to the largest numbers; in practice only the majority has the power to make and unmake governments. It follows that people can live free and at peace only if their society is just.

IV

THE JUST SOCIETY

My notion of justice is the old Aristotelian one: that every individual should receive what is due to him or her. It's simply a question of fairness. At college I realized that some of my classmates had to do their homework on the kitchen table, surrounded by the rest of the family, while I had a room of my own at home. I was always ambitious, I always wanted to be head of the class, but I didn't want to compete with special advantages while my opponents had one hand tied behind their backs. So a just society means equal opportunities.

Saint-Exupéry told a story of travelling by train from France to Poland and seeing on board a little boy, the son of poor immigrants. Maybe this is a Mozart, he thought, but he'd never have the chance to learn an instrument because his parents have nothing to eat. And I used to think of all the wasted potential in the organization of societies that don't give equal opportunities to all. That doesn't mean that everyone should have a piano and be able to play it. It means that everyone should have a chance to fulfil himself or herself according to his or her potential.

Rather than trying to build a society that is founded on concepts of quantity, the governments that I had the honour of leading tried to make more and more of their decisions based on quality. We didn't reject the material values, the civilization of the "more" that brought Canada to a very advanced degree of progress and gave Canadians one of the very highest standards of living in the world. But we were saying that now, having reached the point where there are enough goods and enough technological skills, we should be able to help the less fortunate and trade off some of our material aims and goals for more spiritual, more qualitative values.

26

The aim of life in society is the greatest happiness of everyone, and this happiness is attained only by rendering justice to each person.

27

Freedom is the most important value of a just society, and the exercise of freedom its principal characteristic. Without these, a human being could not hope for true fulfilment – an individual in society could not realize his or her full potential. And deprived of its freedom, a people could not pursue its own destiny – the destiny that best suits its collective will to live.

28

What led me to enter politics in 1965 was not a desire to fight for freedom; in a way, that was already yesterday's battle. In my thinking, the value with the highest priority in the pursuit of a Just Society had become equality. Not the procrustean kind of equality where everyone is raised or lowered to a kind of middle ground. I mean equality of opportunity.

For where is the justice in a country in which an individual has the freedom to be totally fulfilled, but where inequality denies him the means? And how can we call a society just unless it is organized in such a way as to give each his due, regardless of his state of birth, his means, or his health?

29

No one in the society should be entitled to superfluous or luxury goods until the essentials of life are made available to everyone. At first glance, that distribution would appear to obtain in Canada. Thanks to our abundant natural wealth and to the techniques of the industrial era, it no longer seems necessary to trample on one another in the scramble for riches. Consequently, most people take it for granted that every Canadian is assured of a reasonable standard of living. Unfortunately, that is not the case.

I was always concerned, for example, about the injustice done to people living in those parts of Canada where they couldn't make a living or where they had a standard of living that was so far below the norm it just wasn't fair. They didn't have the services from their governments, they didn't have the quality in their schools, they didn't have the opportunity for investment.

In the same way that the Official Languages Act was to create a level playing field between French- and English-speaking Canadians in dealing with their government, the Department of Regional Economic Expansion was to level the field on the economic side, and I gave it to Jean Marchand, my friend and strongest minister. The idea was to create a department that would specialize in the need to attract investment to the poorer parts of the country, so that every individual could be free and equal, not only as regards language, but also as regards economic opportunities.

We had to find the right tools. First we tried to create incentives to bring investment to the less-developed regions. That didn't work all that well, so we tried creating growth centres in the less-developed regions, rather than bringing jobs to every unsustainable village. There were no easy solutions, but we did get some results. Jobs were created; the poverty rate was lowered considerably; and the objective corresponded to my view of Canada that a citizen has a right to expect to lead a decent life in any part of the country. It was necessary in a country as vast and sparsely populated as Canada, and it was a matter of justice.

30

18 The Just Society will be one in which all of our people will have the means and the motivation to participate. The Just Society will be one in which personal and political freedom will be more securely ensured than it has ever been in the past. The Just

Society will be one in which the rights of minorities will be safe from the whims of intolerant majorities. The Just Society will be one in which those regions and groups which have not fully shared in the country's affluence will be given a better opportunity. The Just Society will be one where such urban problems as housing and pollution will be attacked through the application of new knowledge and new techniques. The Just Society will be one in which our Indian and Inuit population will be encouraged to assume the full rights of citizenship through policies which will give them both greater responsibility for their own future and more meaningful equality of opportunity. The Just Society will be a united Canada, united because all of its citizens will be actively involved in the development of a country where equality of opportunity is ensured and individuals are permitted to fulfil themselves in the fashion they judge best.

31

Justice to me is a warm spirit, born of tolerance and wisdom, present everywhere, ready to serve the highest purposes of rational man. To seek to create the just society must be amongst the highest of those human purposes. Because we are mortal and imperfect, it is a task we will never finish; no government or society ever will. But from our honest and ceaseless effort, we will draw strength and inspiration, we will discover new and better values, we will achieve an unprecedented level of human consciousness. On the never-ending road to perfect justice we will, in other words, succeed in creating the most humane and compassionate society possible.

V

TOWARDS A JUST WORLD

32

My approach to international relations was really based on my approach to the Canadian community. The community of mankind should be treated in the same way as you would treat your community of fellow citizens. It was an idealistic approach, as opposed to a realpolitik approach. I felt it was the duty of a middle power like Canada, which could not sway the world with the force of its armies, to at least try to sway the world with the force of its ideals. I wanted to run Canada by applying the principles of justice and equality, and I wanted our foreign policy to reflect similar values.

33

We are living in an age where the only constant factor is rapid change. The question is: Can we harness change in order that our human societies now and in the future be equitably governed, that is to say, so that every human being be enabled to fulfil himself or herself to the utmost? In other words, can mankind develop the self-control and sense of fairness that would permit reason and justice to govern the earth? Or must we forever lament with Emerson that "Things are in the saddle, / And ride mankind"?

34

Having established firmly the principle of the positive freedoms – the freedoms "of" – we now find ourselves involved in a struggle to establish with equal sanctity the negative freedoms – the freedoms "from" – from want, from hunger, from disease, from nuclear holocaust, from environmental degradation.

And we find that this struggle is more complex, more awkward, and more wide-ranging than we had thought possible. There is no single tyrant here; no evil king, no zealot of the Church against whom we can focus our energies and direct our strategies. Equally, there is no immediate and identifiable challenge to our well-being that can be laid low with a single outburst of passion and courage.

35

Never before in history has the disparity between the rich and the poor, the comfortable and the starving, been so extreme; never before have mass communications so vividly informed the sufferers of the extent of their misery; never before have the privileged societies possessed weapons so powerful that their employment in the defence of privilege would destroy the haves and the have-nots indiscriminately. We are faced with an overwhelming challenge. In meeting it, the world must be our constituency.

36

It is hardly credible that nations which have learned that their destinies are linked, that national aims can no longer be wholly realized within national boundaries, that beggaring our neighbours is the surest way of beggaring ourselves, should have discovered no better alternative to maintaining their security than an escalating balance of terror. And it is even less credible that, in a world of finite resources and in so many parts of which basic human needs remain unsatisfied, hundreds of billions of dollars in resources should have to be spent year by year for purposes of security.

37

Security, even absolute security, is not an end in itself. It is only the setting that permits us to pursue our real ends: economic well-being, cultural attainment, the fulfilment of the human personality. But those ends are all incompatible with a world of neighbours armed to the teeth.

38

The role of leadership today is to encourage the embrace of a global ethic. An ethic that abhors the present imbalance in the basic human condition – an imbalance in access to health care, to a nutritious diet, to shelter, to education. An ethic that extends to all human beings, to all space, and through all time. An ethic that is based on confidence in mankind.

39

We must aim for nothing less than an acceptable distribution of the world's wealth. In doing so, the inequities resulting from the accidental location of valuable geological formations should no more be overlooked than should the present unequal acquisition of technological and managerial skills. Nor should we be reluctant in encouraging those willing to help themselves.

40

If we accept, as I presume we do, that the extreme disparity in living standards between the rich and the poor, the comfortable and the hungry, cannot be permitted to continue; if we also accept, as I think we do, that there are benefits which flow from a reduction of the division between states which are developed and those that are developing; if these propositions we accept, then also we must accept some responsibility for their implementation.

41

24

The classical scope of responsibility – to one's own person, to one's family, to one's community and nation – must be broadened. Not even the biblical admonition of responsibility to all human beings is sufficiently broad. The new responsibility must be more. It must extend to all space and through all time. It must be inclusive of persons far beyond our own national frontiers; it must encompass the physical planet and all its ingredients – water and air, non-renewable resources, living organisms; it must extend into the future not just for months or years, but for decades.

42

The twentieth-century devotion to material gain has created an imbalance in the human condition that infects the attitudes of all too many men and women and the policies of most governments. Economic criteria to the exclusion of almost all others are employed as the measurement of individual achievement and of governmental performance. "Prosperity" is the rallying cry of politicians everywhere. But what of happiness? What of contentment? What of satisfaction? Are we to believe that these are concomitants of economic growth?

43

Mankind's technical achievements in the past two hundred years have been breathtaking, but the test of our civilization will be the measure of control to which these achievements are required to submit in order to be at the service of society. Unquestionably, the speed of our accomplishments appears to have outdistanced our ability to fit our technological triumphs within some framework of reason. Is this a permanent condition? Surely not, for if it were, the future of mankind would be doubtful indeed. What has happened is that the undisciplined progression of events, the unpredictable leaps and bounds of technical knowledge passed long ago the rationale for its wise application and use.

44

Technological accomplishment and population growth have both reached such a degree of acceleration that the world at this moment is placed precariously at the commencement of several exponential curves. Going up at a perilous rate are population and pollution; coming down at a rate of equal concern are reserves of natural resources and acreage suitable for cultivation. And we have been deluding ourselves for a quarter of a century with a misleading bookkeeping system that permits industry, and government, and agriculture, and every segment of the community to pass on certain costs to society at large.

45

If the biosphere cannot tolerate further pollution from the third of the world that is industrialized, then surely it cannot absorb simultaneously the same rates of pollution from the other two thirds. If the earth's resources cannot support the present rate of exploitation for the benefit of the minority, then it cannot permit that extraction to be tripled. If assistance and transfers to the developing countries are as yet making little significant impact, considerably more cannot be expected from only a marginal increase in the pattern and quantity of aid. If the developing countries cannot now support the heavy burden of overpopulation, relief will not be found in transferring a few hundreds of thousands of human beings to the more-developed countries.

46

I am not suggesting that business, industry, or for that matter government is engaging in a conscious conspiracy to denude the landscape or cheat the consumer. Neither am I suggesting that civil servants possess somehow the ability to make choices on behalf of the consumer, to balance for society as a whole the advantages and disadvantages of any given industrial process, or even of the introduction of an industry into a natural setting. I do not deny that some government policies appear contradictory, any more than it can be denied that society as a whole harbours contradictions. Thus a community which will not tolerate a government's decision to close a polluting plant, causing hundreds of persons to lose their jobs, will not hesitate for a moment to condemn the same government for its failure to protect the ecology.

47

Perhaps we are caught up in a spiral of circumstance in which our desire for jobs and decent incomes and variety in our lives provides us with no alternative except to lay waste the surface of the earth and to foul the atmosphere. After all, how can one measure the value of a salmon stream, or a species of wildlife, against the benefits of an open-pit mine which will provide jobs for hundreds? How can one compare the pleasures of untouched wilderness with the convenience of a four-lane highway? We seem to have so much untouched space; why not use some of it for people?

There are no easy answers to these questions, for the problems they pose are in many instances contradictory. But that doesn't mean that there are no answers, or that mankind in the past has been unable to come to grips with equally trying dilemmas. Some solutions have been superior to others, in large measure because a sense of wonder and awe has been permitted to exist beside the regimentation of reason.

48

What we face now is not deprivation, but the challenge of sharing. We need not do without, but we must be good stewards of what we have. To ensure nature's continued bounty, we are not asked to suffer, but we are asked to be reasonable. We are asked to adjust our demands to nature's limitations. We are asked to concentrate not on what we have, but on what we are.

49

Fearful though I am of the havoc that will be the inevitable result of continued selfishness and indifference, I am far from despondent, for I believe in the human quality of man's instincts and in the essentially rational behaviour of which he is capable.

Those instincts have lifted him from a solitary hunting animal to an intensely social being, aware of the advantages that flow from co-operation and from the sharing of tasks, aware of the benefits that follow when new structures are set in place to facilitate that co-operation. The history of mankind has been shaped in large measure by men and women who have acted as architects of social organization.

50

What I dare to believe is that men and women everywhere will come to understand that no individual, no government, no nation is capable of living in isolation, or of pursuing policies inconsistent with the interests – both present and future – of others. That self-respect is not self-perpetuating but depends for its existence on access to social justice. That each of us must do all in our power to extend to all persons an equal measure of human dignity – to ensure through our efforts that hope and faith in the future are not reserved for a minority of the world's population, but are available to all.

51

Each of us shares a common desire: to turn over to our children a world safer than the one we inhabit: a world not subject to nuclear blackmail or coercion, a world not frightened by insidious terrorist attacks and not threatened by imbalances in the equilibrium of nature. Nor is this the only desire we share. There is, I know, still another: that in years to come we will be able to face our children and assure them that we did not lack the courage to face these difficult questions, did not lack the stamina to pursue the correct solutions.

VI

ON FREE ENTERPRISE

I had been quite a conventional thinker about economics in my youth. Business was there to produce the goods and services. The state was there to provide the proper environment for the production of wealth. But I had also seen a lot of poverty; I had seen the Depression; I had seen the misery of the Third World. It is fine to create wealth, and it is the job of businessmen to look after their profits, but who looks after the underprivileged, the homeless, the hungry, at home and around the world? So, at Harvard and the London School of Economics and the Sorbonne, I began looking for solutions. And I arrived at a rather conventional balance between the role of the private sector and the role of the state.

Most years, the governments of which I was a part were faced with the choice of trying to balance the budget or dealing with areas of injustice in the country. For if you try to correct all the injustices, you will never balance the budget. Even my most politically inclined advisers weren't interested in throwing money around just to get votes. They did, however, have the traditional liberal view that the problem of finding jobs for people should be solved without worrying about the deficit. That was our priority, to build a just society, and we assumed that the money we spent would be paid down with the swing of the cycle in a few years.

That was neither revolutionary nor unduly optimistic: it was basic Keynesianism, which had worked so well as a balance wheel for so many decades. Keynesianism is shorthand for countercyclical budgeting. In the lean years, when there's high unemployment, instead of trying to raise taxes or cut spending, you run a deficit in order to create work or distribute money. Then, when prosperity returns, you repay the debt. That's why we thought, at the tail end of the Keynesian consensus, that it was proper to run a deficit in hard times in the hopes that we would run a surplus when the good times came around. And we were in hard times, with increasing unemployment, the FLQ crisis, and so on.

Then we were hit by the shocks produced by the sudden and dramatic increase of world oil prices. As a result, we were surprised by a completely new phenomenon unknown to Keynesianism, stagflation, in which we had to fight inflation and unemployment at the same time; and, as it turned out, there was no return to the great rush of growth and prosperity that followed the Second World War. Furthermore, after bringing in all sorts of social programs, we saw that they were costing more than the economic experts thought they would, partly because of the inflationary factor. They were coming unstuck at the same time as our revenues were drying up because of the worldwide recession. Since we weren't getting the swing of the pendulum that Keynesianism had forecast, we couldn't pay back the debt by raising taxes. On the contrary, we were lowering them by indexing them to inflation because the economy was in a down period.

It is obvious that the welfare state can only distribute what is produced, and I have always believed that the market system is the most efficient way of producing wealth. But, after 1974, with inflation growing at a dangerous rate and everyone competing for a larger share of a smaller pie, Canada was technically a poorer country with an unrealistic psychological inclination to want to be as rich as we were before. It wasn't that inflation was destroying our economy, as some believed, but rather that it was further aggravating the uneven distribution of wealth and purchasing power.

I felt that the reasonable opinion-makers in the business class and labour unions should have understood that, if they didn't want inflation, they had to agree to take a smaller share for the time being. But whenever we tried to put a damper on the revolution of rising expectations through meetings and commissions, management said that it wouldn't be able to stay in business if it had to cut profits, while labour refused to accept lower wages.

As I argued at the time, it didn't seem as though we could make even our modified free-market system work to prevent the problem, and it would do no good to try to create a pure free-market economy to solve our future problems, because it won't work either. For stating that obvious truth, I was falsely accused of wanting to kill free enterprise and substitute a system of state control over all economic decisions. Indeed, I made no mention of free enterprise. I spoke about the free market, and there is a difference. Canadians haven't had a free-market economy for over a hundred years. Governments of every political stripe since the days of John A. Macdonald have overseen a mixture of private enterprise and public enterprise, wherein the state entered the marketplace to promote growth and stability, whether through the wheat board or the auto pact.

Traditionally, in fact, business has built Canada with the help of the government. The government was seen as a partner, and so it should be. Thus, I have never believed in nationalization per se *or expropriation. I would describe myself as a middle-of-the-road liberal who believes that the public authorities have to provide counterweights to make sure that private enterprise doesn't, through greed, put everything into one class.*

52

Without a healthy economic climate, we cannot be free to make choices as a nation, cannot provide enough jobs for our workers, cannot assist the less-fortunate peoples of the world. Unless we control the damaging forces of inflation and unemployment, we will lose the benefit of the social progress we have made. Unless we provide an adequate supply of essential commodities, and make sure our economic institutions serve our national goals, we will have less freedom to shape our own future.

53

But how do we get the kind of growth we want, and prevent the kind of growth we don't want? That is the basic question we must answer; and the answer must be worked out not by governments alone, but by a free people working together to determine their own future.

54

Since the seventeenth century, Western civilization had been evolving in a context of boundless opportunity, provided by expanding markets, inexhaustible resources, and technological progress. The aim of the legal machinery was to free man from the fetters left over by medieval institutions, in order that each person might be at liberty to make the most out of the existing environment. Hence the legislators and lawyers were constantly called upon to fashion and to use legal instruments for the protection and development of civil rights and liberties.

Within such a legal framework, Western man reached standards of living undreamed-of three centuries previously. But in the process, he had set up institutions wherein the principle of maximum self-assertion by all was eventually to lead to maximum insecurity for many. Economic Darwinism produced a great increment in the wants and needs of industrial man, but not always the means to fulfil them adequately. More and more, people began to realize that the concept of civil rights availed them little against such realities as economic exploitation or massive unemployment.

55

The principles of *laissez-faire* were undoubtedly instrumental in bringing about the extraordinary growth in wealth which accompanied the industrial revolution. But the industrial revolution, it will be recalled, was hardly a tale of equality and fraternity. In terms of misery, disease, injustice, wanton indignity, and sheer wastage of human lives, it easily surpassed the years of the Terror. Indeed, if a tally could be made in the four quarters of the globe, one wonders if it would not be a match for the tens of millions sacrificed by Stalin in the name of the dictatorship of the proletariat, when he attempted to force the backward Soviet society through its own industrial revolution.

56

I had thought that the Great Depression of the 1930s had destroyed forever the notion that a free-market economy, if unassisted by government, would produce by itself the ideal state of steady economic growth, stable prices, and full employment. The Depression convinced most people of the necessity of government intervention on a broad front, in the interests of overall economic stability. It was also recognized that governments had to intervene in the economy to redistribute income, for example, and to make sure that private industry acted in the public interest.

36

57

There is something quite touching about the abiding faith in the market system shown by all those reformers who are trying to free themselves from the dead hand of central planning. Yet I cannot help but wonder how many of them realize that, even in the best of circumstances, our so-called free markets are not always free, and that even though the market has proved to be the main condition for the efficient production and accumulation of the wealth of nations, it can hardly be claimed that its purpose and effect are to ensure that the distribution of that wealth be either fair or just.

58

Nor can it be held that in our market societies the efficient production of goods and services will guarantee the people's health or the preservation of their environment, or that the slogan "let the consumer decide" produces beneficial choices in those who are manipulated by advertising and conditioned by a society dedicated to acquisitiveness.

59

If the centrally planned economies have failed for having made too little use of the market, our Western capitalist societies are failing because of their too-great reliance on the market. The law of supply and demand is not an objective law found in Nature, like the law of gravity. It's a law whose operation is based on subjective variables such as human decisions and feelings. Absent a social contract whereby people direct their governments to define the conditions and limits of production, distribution, and consumption, the market will simply turn out more of everything desired by those wielding some form of power: more arms for the military, more profits for business, more goods and services for the consumer, to each according to his rank. The market is not equipped to consider and report that, as by-products, it is also producing more misery for the underclasses, more health hazards for the community, more drugs and crime for the cities, more carbon dioxide for the greenhouse effect, more depletion of the ozone layer, more destruction of rainforests and of genetic varieties.

60

No businessman would calculate his net gain without first taking into effect the deterioration of his plant building, the depreciation of his machinery, and the depletion of his stock of raw materials. Why then do Western governments continue to worship at the temple of Gross National Product? Is it not time we paid heed to resource exhaustion, to environmental deterioration, to the social costs of overcrowding, to the extent of solid-waste disposal? Shouldn't we, in short, be replacing our reliance on GNP with a much more revealing figure – a new statistic which might be called Net Human Benefit? And shouldn't governments also challenge more vigorously the current myth that somehow competition

and freedom of choice inevitably protect the interest
of the consumer?

61

The Gross National Product is no measurement of
social justice, or human dignity, or cultural attainment. Yet in the absence of reliable social indicators
we elect governments, formulate foreign policies,
offer advice to the world at large – all on the assumption that economic growth is not only an attribute of
the good life but also is in fact its guarantor.

62

How often in our blindness do we reflect on the fact
that those computers calculating the magical GNP,
measuring as they do prices of items, regard with
equal weight the manufacture of a motor vehicle and
the consequences of a fatal automobile accident,
marriage and divorce, health and sickness, lawful-
ness and crime? The computer does so because GNP
is the total value of goods and services. A museum,
for these purposes, is indistinct from a mortuary so
long as it charges an entrance fee.

63

So indiscriminate are our values that we allow ourselves to be directed by governments on the single
assumption that the expenditure of money is a measure of happiness. Yet what does growth of the GNP
do to confine or reduce the extent of delinquency
in juveniles, corruption in government, monopoly in

business, stagnancy in cultural activity, limitations in educational opportunity, pollution in our environment? What solutions does it offer to the presence of violence, or to the absence of beauty. Bluntly stated, it does nothing. Nevertheless, it is this "nothing" that directs our lives.

64

Economic reform is impossible so long as legislators, lawyers, and businessmen cling to economic concepts which were conceived for another age. The liberal idea of property helped to emancipate the bourgeoisie but it is now hampering the march toward economic democracy. The ancient values of private property have been carried over into the age of corporate wealth. As a result, our laws and our thinking recognize as proprietors of an enterprise men who today hold a few shares which they will sell tomorrow on the stock market; whereas workers who may have invested the better part of their lives and of their hopes have no proprietary right to that job, and may be expropriated from it *without compensation* whenever a strike or lock-out occurs, whenever they grow old, or whenever capital decides to disinvest.

65

That same erroneous concept of property has erected a wall of prejudice against reform, and a wall of money against democratic control. As a consequence, powerful financial interests, monopolies, and cartels are in a position to plan large sectors of the national economy for the profit of the few, rather than for the welfare of all. Whereas any serious planning by the state, democratically controlled, is dismissed as a step towards Bolshevism.

66

Yet if this society does not evolve an entirely new set of values, if it does not set itself urgently to producing those services which private enterprise is failing to produce, if it is not determined to plan its development for the good of all rather than for the luxury of the few, and if every citizen fails to consider himself as the co-insurer of his fellow citizen against all socially engineered economic calamities, it is vain to hope that Canada will ever really reach freedom from fear and freedom from want.

67

Market economies have yet to make a choice between: (a) untrammelled economic growth of the kind that has prevailed until now; (b) sustainable growth; or (c) rejection of the entire growth mystique. If our democracies are enlightened enough to go for choice B or C, the art of government will entail a different kind of planning than that currently practised on the people's behalf by the multinational corporations. And it will certainly necessitate a return to a more regulated economy, where the public interest would have priority over private profits. Thus, true equality of opportunity, for all, regardless of the condition of their birth or the size of their bank account, may some day become the goal of life in civilized societies.

68

The contest between political systems, if not ideologies, is bound to continue. On the one hand, the capitalist countries are still far from having resolved their internal contradictions; and, if this be true in the United States of America, it is even more so in the Koreas, the Brazils, the Chiles, and the South Africas of this world. On the other hand, the centrally planned economies, having at last discovered that progress is no longer possible under totalitarian state planning, must ponder their choices. No doubt some of them will opt for Western-type democracies with free markets, but others will certainly strive to preserve the egalitarian aspirations of collectivism, reconciling the virtues of a free market with a form of democratic planning.

So there is hope that we will continue to live in a pluralistic world for a while yet. And we will continue to struggle with problems raised by Plato and Aristotle, by Rousseau and Locke. How can individuals remain free, yet be restrained by the state? How can the exercise of liberty lead to a society of equals?

VII

THE ROLE OF THE STATE

In Quebec before the Quiet Revolution we were taught to view the state as "a taloned ogre," as I once wrote, "from whom citizens must forcibly wrest their meagre liberties." A couple of decades later neo-conservatives began preaching the same kind of contempt for the state everywhere, with the same unfortunate results: bad citizenship, political immorality, and weak collective action. And, in both situations, business people wanted the state to stand back and let them get on with the business of creating wealth. But economies are also built by the workers, the consumers, the whole population, and freedom tends to create inequality because there are the strong and the weak, the healthy and the sick, the rich and the poor. So, if in the process of creating wealth, business creates inflation or unemployment as well, you obviously need a state to step in as a counterweight in order to regulate the economy by increasing taxes on the wealthy or giving subsidies to the poor or strengthening the power of the consumer.

Furthermore, business likes to say, we don't need the state, keep out of our backyard, we can't compete if governments increase taxes or bring in regulations to

43

help some underprivileged group. But don't they always want trade commissions to open up foreign markets, or bail-outs when their businesses turn bad, or tax breaks to encourage investment? In other words, they want the state to help them when they need help, but not to help the unemployed or the sick. And the same is true of the unions. They may have demanded better labour laws and a cap on corporate profits in the 1970s, but they fought tooth and nail against price and wage controls.

Eventually, we had to introduce such controls, but not because I loved them. In fact, I had campaigned against them during the 1974 election, so even for political reasons I was sorry to have to resort to them. In this case, however, the private sector hadn't made the market work effectively for the good of Canada. And though there may have been instances of "rough justice," as some called it, throughout the life of the controls program, it was nothing like the gross injustices that would have been caused in the absence of controls, by an intolerable rate of inflation.

As it happened, inflation was arrested – whether because of the controls or because the economy would have given that result anyway, nobody can say. But, when it returned in the 1980s, I knew that I couldn't get into the same kind of political wrangle in order to impose controls on the whole economy once again. So I approached the problem by saying, instead of imposing controls on everyone, let us as a government set an example by imposing them on ourselves, by limiting the wage increases in the public service to 6 per cent in year one and 5 per cent in year two. Happily, that also *suited my belief in the sovereignty of the people. We were going to show the people by giving them that leadership, not by forcing them to follow. And it worked, with much less grief and confrontation, when nobody thought it would.*

Of course, in the age of globalization, when capital can move so freely and easily, every state has lost a lot of its sovereignty. (That makes me wonder, by the way, whether an independent Quebec wouldn't have more trouble protecting its sovereignty by itself rather than as part of a bigger country which is a member of the Group of Seven economic powers.) To better protect their citizens, governments increasingly are going to have to act together. In the meantime, I believe there are steps that governments can and should take to help the less fortunate and protect workers.

69

As Aristotle said, people live in society so that they can live a full life. The point of human society is that people living together, by mutual help, co-operation, and the division of labour, can fulfil themselves better than if they lived apart. If men and women could not direct their collective effort to that end, they might as well go off and live all alone in the woods and on the hills.

70

The state is by definition the instrument whereby human society collectively organizes and expresses itself. A sovereign society that fears the state is a moribund society, unconvinced of the usefulness of its own existence.

71

While understanding as well as anyone else the limits of government and the law, the liberal knows that both are powerful forces for good, and does not hesitate to use them.

72

For a liberal, the first role of government is to create the conditions for, and to remove obstacles to, individual and collective freedoms. Laws and leadership are our weapons. Poverty, ignorance, inequality, and the exploitation of the weak by the strong have always been our enemies.

73

There's no longer a belief in the absolute liberal state. It is giving way to an interventionist state which intervenes to make sure that the strong and the powerful don't abuse their strength and their power in order to take freedoms away from the little man.

74

We believe in individual freedom, but we believe that when majorities oppress minorities or the rich oppress the poor or the strong oppress the weak, "no government" is bad government, because the state should be there to protect the weak against the strong.

I'm not saying that the state can resolve all our problems; I'm saying that some problems are better resolved by the state than by Adam Smith's invisible hand. Freedom is not licence. Freedom entails responsibility. And if you believe in liberalism, you seek to fight all those who try to curtail liberty. If the times indicate that you need to exercise more control of the powerful in order to permit more flourishing of liberty in all other areas, then liberalism hasn't fallen back, it has advanced.

75

The state is neither a supernatural power that unleashes irresistible plagues upon us nor an ogre that gobbles up families and crucifixes. In any stable, self-governing society, the state is simply a creation, emanating from the members of that society. In other words, the state is precisely what the people want it to be, and has only such reality as they choose to give it. Its authority is limited by the general agreement to obey it. And it can exert only as much force as the citizens lend it.

76

We live in society precisely so that we can tackle collectively the problems that we cannot solve individually.

77

When the day came that neither the individual nor private enterprise could provide the bridges and roads needed for travel, organize the police and fire brigades required for public safety, or devise the water and sewage systems necessary for hygiene, the community simply decided to solve these problems communally, through the state. And nobody dreamt of crying "Communism!"

Now, what the state could do for sewers, could it not do in other realms where individuals by themselves cannot provide the answer? If the state can organize a fire brigade to protect our goods, why should it not organize a teaching brigade to develop our minds, or knock down slums to protect our way of life?

78

Technology, which brings abundance and material happiness, presupposes an undifferentiated mass of consumers; it also tends to minimize the values that let a human being acquire and retain his own identity, values that I am grouping here under the vague term "cultural." The political order created by the state must struggle against this kind of depersonalization by pursuing cultural objectives.

The state must use its legal powers to compel the economic community to favour certain values that would otherwise be destroyed by the pressure of economic forces. In other words, just as the state intervenes in economic matters to protect the weak through social legislation, so it must intervene to ensure the survival of cultural values in danger of being swamped by a flood of dollars.

79

Even this kind of cultural investment is only achieved at a cost, not only economic, but also cultural. For it supposes that the state knows better than the citizen what is "good" for him or her culturally, and such a hypothesis must always be applied with utmost prudence and consideration. More than any other, this kind of value is international and common to all people; in the long term, then, the state should ideally promote an open culture. There is also a danger that cultural protection, like its economic counterpart, would tend eventually to produce a weak, "hothouse" culture.

That's why, with regard to culture, our government had no intention of dropping a cultural iron curtain across the U.S. border. I've never believed that the best way to develop any culture is to lock it in a ghetto. Rather, we sought to strengthen Canada's identity and control in an open, outward-looking spirit, one that welcomed the best from outside and allowed it to compete with – but not subsume – that which is identifiably Canadian. Whether supporting our artists and scholars or promoting Canadian films and music, I didn't feel any great conflict between such efforts to develop our national identity and the open, universalist cultural attitude inherent in liberalism.

49

80

Will anyone think I am preaching statism? On the contrary, I am preaching the doctrine of the servant state. For if I say today that the state should do more in the name of the community it is only after repeatedly saying that no political authority has an unconditional right to exist. I want the state to do more, but only after we have stopped thinking of it as an absolute master. In fact, if we were to extend the powers of the state without having multiplied our means of controlling its policy and limiting its methods of acting, we would tend to increase our enslavement. That is why I am wary of those who preach indiscriminate nationalization without setting themselves first to undermine the undue majesty of political power.

81

A state enlightened in this way can then play its part, which is to protect the rights of every individual, and especially of the weak. This function of the state is indispensable above all in a modern society like ours, where the citizen is in greater danger of becoming enmeshed in a network of extremely complicated social, economic, and administrative institutions. An ordinary citizen has neither the time nor the means to make sure whether a certain public utility is charging him fair rates, whether a certain monopoly is selling to him at reasonable prices, whether a certain cartel or a certain company is not exploiting him to death. And even if the citizen knew that he was the victim of injustice he would not have the power to attack the guilty.

82

If the citizens want to avoid being ordered about against their will, they must provide themselves with a protector in the form of a state strong enough to subordinate to the public good all the individuals and organisms that go to make up society.

VIII

ON DEMOCRACY

Even in my days as an intellectual, I wrote against violence and argued for reason. I may have walked in a few demonstrations to get some justice for a cause, but I never supported terrorism in any way. We had a democratic society. We could change our leaders. Violence is not proof of high moral conscience; it's not proof of the rectitude of the ideas. It's proof of the low respect in which terrorists hold the rest of the society. They think that people are so stupid and so corrupt and so twisted in their minds that it's no use preaching the truth to them, that they're not clever enough or informed enough to choose the "truth" that the terrorists have chosen. This is the seed of totalitarianism and dictatorship.

It's perhaps difficult when you're in a minority to have your point of view accepted. But the fact that you are in a minority means that the majority holds a different view. It may be wrong, it may be misinformed, but if each man claims to know better than the majority what is good for it, then he takes into his own hands the right to destroy the society and break its laws. In these circumstances, the majority has the right to defend itself. As long as there is freedom of speech, and as long as everyone is free to form opposition parties and dissident groups, there is no place for violence.

That's why I refused to deal with the FLQ's long list of demands in October 1970. If we had to release common criminals who had been found guilty of manslaughter and murder every time someone had been kidnapped, there'd be no end to it. For, if we ever caught the kidnappers, we'd have to release them too in order to get the latest kidnap victim freed, and so on. And, because of my belief in democracy, I was offended that some gang of terrorists was trying to establish itself as an alternative government. If you're a government, your first duty is to govern. Whether you govern well or badly can be discussed later, but you have to maintain order. You can't let unelected people wielding guns exercise the authority over who should be in jail and who shouldn't.

It is an abdication of responsibility for a government to be hospitable to anarchy. By so doing, it contributes to a climate of fear, encourages negative manifestations of the human instinct for survival, and invites tribalism and lawlessness. In that kind of environment there is no safety, no order, and no protection for the unpopular, for the minorities, or for the weak.

Nor do I believe that elected representatives should abdicate their responsibility by being nothing but the mouthpieces for their constituencies. In its extreme form this ceases to be representative democracy and becomes direct democracy. Though it may look more democratic, it's really tantamount to saying that policies and laws must be decided by the people themselves coming to grips with their problems; policies and laws must be decided in the streets by the masses. It's a misunderstanding of parliamentary democracy, and it cannot be made to work in large societies, because small groups meeting to deal with very important problems from their regional or local point of view cannot have in mind the legalistic, administrative, constitutional functions of government that are the fabric society must have to function in an orderly way.

Direct democracy is not a progressive form of democracy. If you try to let everybody make the decisions, you'll have complete anarchy. Even the Greeks discovered two and a half thousand years ago that they needed smaller groups of people to execute the decisions. Participatory democracy means that you have a chance to have your ideas known to those who govern you. It doesn't mean that the government must always decide the way you think it should. You participate, the government decides, then you judge its decisions at election time.

83

The liberal person marks a juncture in human evolution; a point at which social change through violence has become morally unacceptable to many, many people. Violence is a negation of individual rights, and respect for those rights is compatible only with gradual social change through selective and deliberate evolution. No other form of change is worthy of people who have evolved, through liberal thought, to that level where a growing proportion of mankind claims to function.

84

The liberal believes in persuasion and the civil dialogue because he believes in democracy itself, for democracy cannot be served by means which deny, and eventually destroy, democratic principles.

85

Both liberty and democracy, in order to exist, require the other. Neither can survive, moreover, without some ability to defend itself against those who would destroy it. The threat is not always, indeed it is seldom, from external sources. It comes on one occasion from the criminal, on another from the wealthy; at one time it will be the intransigence of the bureaucracy, on another the cleverness of politicians. Democracy and liberty must face sometimes the hysteria of a mob and at other times the calculated plans of a handful of conspirators. They are constantly under the attack of the bigoted and stupid; on occasion they need protection from the overrighteous and the superpatriotic. If anything be certain, it is that the continued vitality of neither liberty nor democracy can be assumed.

86

The liberal state is an open and democratic state, because it trusts its citizens. But for liberalism to thrive, the citizens must also trust the democratic state to protect their rights and freedoms – even, when necessary, by using force to defend itself against violence from those who abuse its trust.

87

Democracy is superior to other political systems because it solicits the express agreement of the people and thus avoids the necessity of violent changes. At each election, in fact, the people assert their liberty by deciding what government they will consent to obey.

88

We must shun the concept of the state as a machine to command obedience and impose order. The truly democratic state should rather *court* obedience and serve the citizens' loyalty by maintaining an order that they will think just. Under these conditions the exercise of force (army, police, prison) cannot become a *habit* of government. My idea of a state "made to measure" applies thoroughly here: the state must use force only to the extent that individuals or organizations try to use it themselves against the common good. If it is true that in the last analysis the state must retain the monopoly of force, the purpose is less to use it than to prevent someone else from usurping its thunderbolts.

89

Democracy need have no fear of open confrontation, for it is strengthened by the exposure of its weaknesses. Democracy does require, however, an atmosphere of honesty in order to flourish. Honesty, in turn, presupposes freedom of choice, not an absence of choice as a result of terror.

90

What I have sought for years in my opposition to those who support violence is some evidence amongst them of a radical intellectual dignity. Those who advocate violence as a means of attaining greater freedom within a democracy are suffering from a fearful misconception: that there is somehow a conflict between man's instincts for justice for his fellows and liberty for himself. Rational men and women know in their hearts that this is not so. It is the task of government to demonstrate to militants of both right and left that there is no conflict, that justice and liberty must co-exist in a single community. But it is also the task of governments to preserve for all citizens their freedoms – from assault, from fear, from illegal acts of all kinds. The authority of democratic governments to protect their citizens finds its legitimacy in the will of the people.

91

The detractors of democracy are wrong, then, in equating this form of government with anarchy, disorder, and impotence. The democratic state is a strong state; but its strength, being based on agreement, can be exerted only in the direction desired by the consensus of citizens.

92

Everywhere in the modern world strong states and competent administrations are required. But, once given these, democracy regains its advantage, for it alone offers the means of using this strength and this competence always for the general good and not for a special interest.

93

Democracy tends towards the good of the community by encouraging each citizen and each group of citizens to protest against the defects of society and to demand justice.

94

At all times and under all systems there is a tendency for the few to use the state to enslave the many. For this, too, democracy appears to be the only possible remedy, since it is the system in which the citizen consents to be governed by a body of laws that the *majority* of citizens wanted.

95

It is convenient to choose governments and pass laws by majority vote, so that those who exercise authority can feel assured of having more supporters than opponents – which is in itself some guarantee that the social order will be upheld. It is true that from one point of view the majority convention is only a roundabout way of applying the law of the stronger, in the form of the law of the more numerous. Let us

admit it, but note at the same time that human group-
ings took a great step towards civilization when they
agreed to justify their actions by counting heads
instead of breaking them.

96

That is not to say that democracy is a perfect form of
government: you just have to look around you. What
holds us to democracy is not that it is faultless but
that it is less faulty than any other system. If the
people use their sovereignty badly, the remedy is not
to take it away from them (for to whom could we
hand it over who would offer a better guarantee for
all citizens?), but rather to educate them to do better.
To be precise, democracy is the only form of government that fully respects the dignity of human beings,
because it alone is based on the belief that all men
and women can be made fit to participate, directly or
indirectly, in the guidance of the society of which
they are members.

97

Democracy genuinely demonstrates its faith in
people by letting itself be guided by the rule of 51 per
cent. For if all men and women are equal, each one
the possessor of a special dignity, it follows inevitably
that the happiness of fifty-one people is more
important than that of forty-nine; it is normal, then,
that – *ceteris paribus* and taking account of the invi-
olable rights of the minority – the decisions preferred by the fifty-one should prevail. But the majority

convention has only a practical value, I repeat. Democracy recognizes that one person may be right and ninety-nine wrong. That is why freedom of speech is sacred: the one person must always have the right to proclaim *his* or *her* truth in the hope of persuading the ninety-nine to change their point of view.

That's also why, if it's a very important decision that can't be easily reversed, such as the independence of Quebec, the majority had better be a substantial one. Otherwise, you will have half a society on one side and half on the other, and the consequence will be perpetual instability. For the sake of stability, therefore, democratic law doesn't always accept the rule of 51 per cent.

98

Parliamentary democracy I take to be a method of governing free people which operates roughly as follows: organized parties that wish to pursue – by different means – a common end, agree to be bound by certain rules according to which the party with the most support governs on condition that leadership will revert to some other party whenever the latter's means become acceptable to the greater part of the electorate. The common end – the general welfare – which is the aim of all parties may be more or less inclusive, and may be defined in different ways by different people. Yet it must in some way include equality of opportunity for everyone in all important fields of endeavour; otherwise "agreement on fundamentals" would never obtain. For instance, democracy cannot be made to work in a country where a large part of the citizens are by status condemned to a perpetual state of domination, economic or otherwise. Essentially, a true democracy must permit the periodic transformation of political minorities into majorities.

IX

ON PARTICIPATION

Participation really means explaining our problems to ourselves. When I talked about participation and participatory democracy, some people thought I meant that every citizen, or at least most of them, should be preoccupied with government every day, that there should be a constant interchange between the elected and the electors. But that can't happen all the time. Instead, we have organized parties and other vehicles for expressing our concerns.

For that purpose, our government tried to build the Liberal party into a mass party – one in which constituencies weren't cornered by the so-called old guard who kept re-electing the same member who, in turn, kept protecting the old guard. We tried to open the party to all dissenters so they would be able to get involved in the policy conferences and constituency teach-ins. And we introduced major electoral reforms to encourage participation and counterbalance the influence of money.

Because of my theory of countervailing powers, I thought the opposition and the government's own MPs should be strong. We gave them the proper tools: private offices, word processors, free travel, money for research. We really believed that the MPs were the creative process through which laws were made and the public was represented. So, aside from the shouting matches and fighting words, we made it a modern instrument of governing.

And, again because I believed in creating counterweights, I wanted to give a voice to those who had no voice. Our society welcomes dissent, it leaves room for dissent, and it's on this basis that ideas and policies are developed. Those who don't agree have a right, indeed they have a duty towards their own consciences, to express their feelings and to draw the attention of the authorities to the particular injustices or inequities about which they feel strongly. Our society needs this. And it would be a danger to our society if too many people were to feel that they can't express their dissent, or don't have the tools for changing the orientation of society, while those in power have microphones and television and the press and so on.

That's why I thought the government should give public funds to those who lacked the tools to advance their own economic and social situations, just as we gave public funds to the opposition parties. We set up various mechanisms for putting money into the hands of native leaders. We created the Royal Commission on the Status of Women and Opportunities for Youth. We instituted "regional desks" in the Prime Minister's Office, not to make it presidential, but to keep me informed about problems across the country. We kept the people better informed by televising the parliamentary debates and establishing Information Canada to make government documents more readily available to the press and public. We consulted Canadians via white papers and town-hall meetings.

99

What is it that the citizens desire? That is the question that every democratic government must ask itself constantly. And it is in this respect that the democratic state, better than any other, turns to account the creative liberty of people living in society. For if it is to establish an order that citizens will agree to support, the state must go further than merely investigating their needs; it must also encourage them to demand what they consider just. In this way democracy becomes a system in which all citizens *participate* in government: the laws, in a sense, reflect the wishes of the citizens and thus turn to account the special wisdom of each one; the social order to some extent embodies all the wealth of human experience that the citizens possess.

100

In such a state the liberty of citizens is an end in itself. The authorities don't think of it as an annoying phrase; on the contrary, they want it, and encourage it as the surest guide to the common good.

To put it another way, decision-making must encourage and reflect the participation of as many citizens as possible. Government must be brought closer to the people and made more sensitive to their needs and aspirations. And the integrity of the individual must be preserved in a society that demands and requires a complex bureaucracy and organization.

101

Plato said: "The cost of not showing an interest in public affairs, is to be governed by persons worse than oneself."

Actually, there are two kinds of active involvement in public affairs: outside involvement, which consists of critically examining the ideas, institutions, and people who, together, compose the political reality; and inside involvement, the result of becoming a politician oneself.

The people who choose the first option and play the role of political critics have to develop their thoughts to the limit. They would quickly lose their independence, and especially their usefulness, if they stopped to consider the enemies they might make by speaking out, or the doors that their words would close to them.

102

It is not enough to avoid evil; we also have to do good. A church would be an impostor if it stayed forever in the catacombs. Similarly, in politics, you cannot stay below ground too long. An excess of unhappiness will snuff out the spirit, and heroic resistance will degenerate into beast-like stubbornness. That unfortunately is what happens to some peoples who have struggled too much, and take virtue itself to be a negation.

103

The problems of organizing society are really problems of getting men and women to agree to the social contract, which really means getting them to accept the basic premises on which the society is founded. And they won't accept those premises unless they understand the rationale for them, and unless they have been given the opportunity to think them through thoroughly.

104

The problems of government are in people's minds, they are in the choices people make. And unless governments put these choices to the people, the revolution of rising expectations will destroy our society. Because citizens will ask more from their government than they are prepared to put into it in the form of taxes, and they will do this not only as citizens as regards the state, they will do it as workers as regards their industry, they will do it as shareholders as regards their company – and the whole society will be destroyed. The main purpose of government today is getting citizens to realize what their priorities must be. And explaining to them the choices they have to make.

105

Parliamentary government does not require a decision from its subjects on each of the technical problems presented by the complicated art of government in the modern world. It would be a delusion to look to a vote of the citizens to settle the details of, for example, a fiscal policy, a war budget, or a diplomatic mission. The citizens as a group can judge such measures only by their effects – real or apparent – on the happiness of the group.

That is why modern democracies hardly ever resort to the plebiscite – which requires each citizen to decide on what is often too technical a question. In contrast, the electoral system asks of the citizens only that they should decide on a set of ideas and tendencies, and on people who can hold them and give effect to them. These sets of ideas and people constitute political parties, which are indispensable for the functioning of parliamentary democracy.

Ultimately, in parliamentary democracies, the decisions must always be taken by the representatives of the people. I am not a believer in parallel authorities or illegitimate authorities. I do not believe that foreign policy can be made in the streets or that policy of any kind should be determined by masses or mobs. I have the strongest disapproval for those who think that, by pressure, by making enough noise, by waving enough signs, they can make the decisions. They should influence the decisions. Their input should be received. But the government obviously cannot do what everyone wants it to do. It has to make what it believes, on balance, is the best choice. Then it's up to the citizens to throw it out if its choices are not satisfactory.

106

To have accountability, to have participatory democracy, you must have exchange of information, you must have the government telling you on what it is basing itself in deciding its policies, and you must have knowledge by the government of what the people want of it as expressed through its riding associations or various contacts with the people. You need these elements, but then the governments must decide and be judged at the end of the term on whether by and large they governed well for the society or not.

X

THE ART OF GOVERNING

The art of governing has some parallels with the art of canoeing, with the movement of the water representing the people, their needs and wants. Sometimes you have to fight against the current. Sometimes you have to shoot the rapids, by going faster than the moving water or back-paddling a bit until you find the most appropriate course between the rocks. Sometimes you get dumped. If you just want to administer things, you let the polls tell you where the river is and then you follow it wherever it goes. But drifting is not really governing. If you want to govern people, you have to choose a path in the river, you have to avoid the rocks, you have to know which rapids you can shoot and which you must portage. There may be risks and dangers. There will be all kinds of decisions to make all the time, but you have to take your canoe where you think it should go if you want to make progress and reach your destination.

We were governing people, I used to tell my party and caucus, we weren't there just to administer things. Anybody could manage the country more or less as well as we could. We were there to give it direction, to lead people in the direction we thought was right. And it was better to be defeated eventually, if we had to be, for having tried to introduce too many changes for the better than to be left behind when the people were moving on.

In economic and social matters we tried to deal with issues before they became crises. When there was massive unemployment, we improved the unemployment benefits. When there were young people who couldn't get a job, we created the Opportunities for Youth program. And when the Parti Québécois was elected in 1976, we tried to make sure that the political uncertainties didn't result in economic regression, hence higher unemployment, hence more people ready to denounce democracy and the federal government.

107

We are confronted by the ageless paradox that certain kinds of freedom, such as the freedom to pursue excellence, are impossible without rules. We limit one kind of freedom in order to promote another. The wisest among us impose rules with a light touch.

108

The great strength of the Liberal Party of Canada in the past has been its ability to achieve a balance between the ambitions of the strong and the needs of the weak, between the strength of organized groups and the rights of the individuals, between the power of the majorities and the liberties of minorities.

109

We are a party of the radical centre. And that means that sometimes we have to fight against the state lest its monopoly withdraw too many liberties from citizens, and sometimes we have to give more power to the state lest men and women and their inequality of brains and of physique come to dominate others and not permit justice and equality to survive with liberty.

110

To me liberalism is not a doctrine. Liberalism is a way of thinking, a way of approaching problems to make sure that the individual gets the maximum of respect and hopefully as great an amount of equality of opportunity in Canada, and in the world, as possible.

111

The liberal's moderation in attitude actually arises, I believe, from the liberal philosophy itself. It springs from a realization that today's problems are complex, and that simple and sloganeering answers can almost certainly be assumed not to be valid ones. The liberal, therefore, is a moderate and not a simplist in expression and conduct primarily because he is a moderate and not a simplist in his concept of society. He is, in brief, a realist, who knows that values change slowly, and knows that in order to change social values one has to change a large complex of ideas and mores.

When I was an academic, involved in intellectual thinking, I felt it my responsibility to state the absolute truth as I saw it, without pulling any punches. But when I got into politics, I learned that you can't seek the absolute truth, because there are so many countervailing forces and you can't be so far ahead of them that they won't follow. So politics became the art of the possible, as the well-known expression puts it. I don't think I ever compromised any of my basic principles, but at times I went a bit slower on one thing and a bit faster on something else in order to remain in government.

Thus, as an intellectual, I may have had a right or duty to say that the notwithstanding clause ought not to have gone into the Charter. As a politician, however, I had to choose between a flawed charter or no charter at all. There was a quid pro quo, in other words, in which the federal government gained something it thought was important for the country in exchange for something the provincial premiers wanted.

In contrast, even as a politician, I could never have accepted either the Meech Lake or the Charlottetown accord. They were totally flawed, in my judgement, because they threatened to transform Canada irreversibly from a balanced federation to a decentralized confederation without offering the federal government anything at all. The result would have been a seriously weakened country in which the Canadian government was subservient to the provinces in appointing senators and justices of the Supreme Court and at the mercy of the Quebec government through the distinct-society clause.

112

The liberal is an optimist at heart, who trusts people. He does not see man as an essentially perverse creature, incapable of moral progress and happiness. Nor does he see him as totally or automatically good. He prizes man's inclinations to good, but knows they must be cultivated and supported.

113

In the short run, a party could maintain itself in power by responding to each crisis as it arose. But if it concentrated only on immediate solutions, it would be ignoring the underlying conditions which caused each crisis. It would be prescribing for the symptoms rather than the disease. Eventually the crises would accumulate and overwhelm the party. A party's particular concern should not be how to settle a particular strike – let the minister of labour and the cabinet worry about that. It should be to resolve the continuing crisis in industrial relations by working out a better system of reconciling the interests of labour, management, and the public. The task is not only more difficult, it is much more important.

114

The state cannot and must not make laws that do not tally by and large with what the citizens want; if it does, they will defy its laws, until the time comes to overthrow it. The real purpose of laws, then, is to educate the citizens in the common good, and persuade them to behave in the public interest, rather than to command and constrain.

115

The true statesman is not one who gives orders to his fellow-citizens so much as he is one who devotes himself to their service. True, one sometimes hears it said that such a man "serves by ruling," but that is not my view. In a constitutional society it is not men, but rather laws, that control us. The rulers are themselves subject to the laws, and they can exert authority only as far as the law allows. Our obedience, then, is not to individuals but to the general will of the nation, a will embodied in laws, to whose service and execution the rulers are appointed.

I was sometimes accused of fostering a presidential style of governing, in large part because of the size and strength of the Prime Minister's Office. But it grew out of the fact that, in a modern and complex society, I needed to keep myself as informed as my ministers about what they were doing, what decisions the cabinet should take collectively, and what the political implications were. That was an improvement, I thought, over the days when the central government appeared weak and confused, and I never feared it would lead to a presidential system. Unlike an American president, for instance, a prime minister is always dependent on having a cohesive cabinet and caucus. If too many of his colleagues resign, he will cease to be prime minister.

Nevertheless, because of television or the insecure times, many people tend to personalize politics, identify with leaders, and seek someone up there telling them what to do – the Moses complex. But I've always insisted that the best way to serve democracy is not to judge leaders on their image or style – whether they're dull or a swinger, born poor or rich, with long hair or short – but on their ideas and their performance.

116

We should start, then, by banishing from our political mores the whole concept that a prime minister *gives* bridges, roads, schools to his province. These are works that society needs, that it gives to itself and pays for through taxes. A prime minister gives nothing at all (unless it is his superfluous services); quite simply, he works in the service of the state as an instrument through which society *gives to itself.*

117

Either a region needs a bridge, a road, a school, or it doesn't. If it doesn't need them, the statesman has no right to promise them. If it does need them, he has no right to refuse them.

118

The statesman may well think differently from his fellow-citizens on certain subjects, he can try to convey his special wisdom to them; but in the final analysis it is the general will that must prevail, not his own will. That is why the statesman must be attentive to the needs of all sectors of society, with no bias towards thwarting any of them, and must wish only to reconcile them all and direct them towards the general interest.

XI

ON HUMAN RIGHTS

119

Certain political rights are inseparable from the very essence of democracy: freedom of thought, speech, expression (in the press, on the radio, etc.), assembly, and association. Indeed, the moment these freedoms suffer the smallest restraint, the citizens have lost their full power to participate in the organization of the social order. And so that each citizen may feel the benefit of the inalienable right to exercise his liberties – in spite of anyone, in spite of the state itself – to these rights two more must be added: equality of all before the law, and the right not to be deprived of one's liberty or one's goods without recourse to a trial before one's peers, under an impartial and independent judicial system.

These rights are so basic that they are regarded in democratic philosophy as inalienable – that is, to assure the effective participation of all citizens in the development of public policy, these rights must remain vested in each citizen independently of the laws. To guarantee that they will remain beyond the reach of the state, many democratic constitutions have felt the need to include a "bill of rights," treating these rights as in some sense anterior to the very existence of the state.

120

The Constitution Act was proclaimed on April 17, 1982. Essentially, it enshrined the values which, back in 1968, I had defined as those that should be respected in the constitution of a Just Society. First, the principle of equal economic opportunity. Secondly, the principle of equality of French and English in all domains of federal jurisdiction. It is important to stress that these two goals were conducive to a conception of the country as a place in which all Canadians were working together to make it strong and united. It would even be correct to say that these goals were the spearheads of our political action at a moment in Canadian history when the centrifugal forces were more potent than the centripetal, and were threatening to break the country apart.

121

The Canadian Charter of Rights and Freedoms went much further, of course. In the grand tradition of the 1789 Declaration of the Rights of Man and the Citizen and the 1791 Bill of Rights of the United States of America, it implicitly established the primacy of the individual over the state and all government institutions, and in so doing, recognized that all sovereignty resides in the people. In this respect, the Canadian Charter was a new beginning for the

Canadian nation: it sought to strengthen the country's unity by basing the sovereignty of the Canadian people on a set of values common to all, and in particular on the notion of equality among all Canadians.

122

A constitutionally entrenched charter seemed the best tool for breaking the ever-recurring deadlock between Quebec and the rest of Canada. If certain language and educational rights were written into the constitution, along with other basic liberties, in such a way that *no* government – federal or provincial – could legislate against them, French Canadians would cease to feel confined to their Quebec ghetto, and the spirit of separatism would be laid to rest forever.

123

The paradox is real: freedom for some is detrimental to the equality of others. And it has been the subject of many philosophical dissertations. How can we prevent strong individuals from using their superior strength to create economic, social, and institutional conditions in which the weak cannot find equal opportunities?

The state may restrain the exercise of a freedom by some if this exercise negates a freedom for others. In other words, the state may limit one individual's freedom if it is necessary (economically, socially, linguistically ...) to enable others to enjoy theirs. In this way, the concepts of society and of the common good have a place in the application of a charter that is intrinsically centred on the freedom and equality of individuals.

It places the onus on whoever invokes such a restraining law to show that the restraint is reasonable and justified in a free and democratic society. It is therefore wrong to pretend that the existence of the Charter is in contradiction with the supremacy of Parliament, and that it replaces the people's representatives with judges who are appointed for life.

124

The very adoption of a constitutional charter is in keeping with the purest liberalism, according to which all members of a civil society enjoy certain fundamental, inalienable rights and cannot be deprived of them by any collectivity (state or government) or on behalf of any collectivity (*nation*, ethnic group, religious group, or other). To use Maritain's phrase, they are "human personalities," they are beings of a moral order – that is, free and equal among themselves, each having absolute dignity and infinite value. As such, they transcend the accidents of place and time, and partake in the essence of universal Humanity. They are therefore not coercible by any ancestral tradition, being vassals neither to their race, nor to their religion, nor to their condition of birth, nor to their collective history.

XII

ON COLLECTIVE RIGHTS

125

Within any given state, individuals may gather together in ethnic, linguistic, religious, professional, political, or other collectivities, and delegate to this or that collectivity the task of promoting their collective interests. And since, in a democracy, governments receive their powers from the people by majority vote at elections, what is to prevent a majority from riding roughshod over the rights of a minority?

The answer, of course, is the Charter of Rights and Freedoms and the Constitution. They do this generally, by enshrining the rights of the individual members within minorities; but in certain instances, where the rights of individuals may be indistinct and difficult to define, they also enshrine some collective rights of minorities.

In other words, the free human being can gather like-minded people to obtain something collectively from the state. That's the way the state works. But it's always the individual who is calling for the formation of the group, and it's always the individuals within the group who possess the rights. The proof is that nobody can be forced to remain in the group.

126

Only the individual is the possessor of rights. A collectivity can exercise only those rights it has received by delegation from its members; it holds them in trust, so to speak, and on certain conditions. Thus, the state, which is the supreme collectivity for a given territory, and the organs of the state, which are the governments, legislatures, and courts, are limited in the exercise of their functions by the Charter and the Constitution in which the Charter is enshrined.

127

What we were seeking was for the individual himself to have the *right* to demand his choice of French or English in his relationships with the federal government, and the *right* to demand a French or English education for his children from a provincial government. And the individual himself would have access to the courts to enforce these rights.

This is not to say that we were denying the importance of a linguistic community in the defence and advancement of the language spoken by its members. However, it seemed clear to us that these matters would never be settled unless the *individual* language rights of each person were enshrined in the constitution of the country, since the English-speaking community would always outnumber the French-speaking in Canada.

128

The spirit and substance of the Charter is to protect the individual against tyranny – not only that of the state but also any other to which the individual may be subjected by virtue of his belonging to a minority group.

129

If we had tried to identify each of the minorities in Canada in order to protect all the characteristics that made them different, not only would we have been faced with an impossible task, but we would shortly have been presiding over the balkanization of Canada. The danger inherent in this would have been particularly acute in the case of minorities that are in a position to be identified with a given territory, like the Celts in Nova Scotia, the Acadians in New Brunswick, the French Canadians in Quebec, and the Indians and Inuit in the Far North.

130

We can go on treating the Indians as having a special status; we can go on adding bricks of discrimination around the ghetto in which they live and, at the same time, perhaps helping them preserve certain cultural traits and certain ancestral rights; or we can say, "You're at a crossroads, the time is now to decide whether the Indians will be a race apart in Canada or whether they will be Canadians of full status." And this is a difficult choice. It must be a very agonizing choice to the Indian peoples themselves. Because, on the one hand, they realize that if they come into the society as total citizens, they will be equal under the law but they risk losing certain of their traditions, certain aspects of their culture, and perhaps even certain of their basic rights.

131

I don't think that we should encourage the Indians to feel that their treaties should last forever within Canada so that they'll be able to receive their twine and their gunpowder. They should eventually become Canadians as all other Canadians and if they are prosperous and wealthy they will be treated like the prosperous and wealthy and they will be paying taxes for the other Canadians who are not so prosperous and not so wealthy, whether they be Indians or English Canadians or French Canadians or Maritimers, and this is the only basis on which everyone in our society can develop as equals.

132

Under the Charter, all Canadians stand as equals before the state. But Quebec's *nationalist* élites, who are fearless in the face of competition from the United States and even the whole world, are scared stiff of English Canada. Only in the Saint-Jean-Baptiste parade are we a *nation* of giants; when the next day dawns and we come to measure ourselves against other Canadians as individuals, we are afraid we are not equal but inferior to them, and we run and hide behind our "collective" rights, which, if need be, we invoke to override the fundamental rights of "others." But what politician or academic or business person will tell us which collectivity is supposed to have those rights?

Is it the French-Canadian collectivity living here and there across Canada? Of course not, since the preponderant ideology in Quebec doesn't give a fig about bilingualism in Canada, and Quebec has gone to bat in court for Alberta and Saskatchewan when they have denied French rights acquired even before these provinces joined Confederation in 1905.

Is it the collectivity of all Quebeckers, then? No, because that collectivity is called a province, and the powers of the province as a collectivity were explicitly recognized long ago by the Constitution Act of 1867.

So it can only be some distinct collectivity within Quebec – but which? Certainly not the members of the anglophone collectivity, since Quebec law denies them any collective rights in relation to signs and certain aspects of education. We can rule out the native peoples, too, since they have been clearly given to understand that they cannot be a distinct society with the right to self-determination because the term has been reserved by Quebeckers of another race.

When the *nationalists* talk about protecting collective rights, then, they are thinking only of French-speaking Quebeckers. But are we sure we know what that means? There are plenty of anglophones who speak very good French and plenty of francophones of various cultural backgrounds who speak languages other than French. Will they all get protection of their collective rights at least for the French-speaking part of their being? If so, what will these rights consist of?

Can Haitian Quebeckers, for instance, protect certain aspects of their own culture by claiming protection as part of the French-speaking collectivity? Or are they excluded from the "unique culture" which Quebec will have the power to promote through derogations from the Charter? Can neo-Canadian Quebeckers of whatever origin choose to renounce their heritage and origins so as to share with "old stock" Quebeckers the protection sought by the French-speaking collectivity? Or are we dealing with a frankly racist notion that makes second- and third-class citizens of everyone but "old stock" Quebeckers?

There are no certainties here, but what does seem clear is that it will not be for the individual to decide whether he or she belongs to the collectivity of "old stock" Quebeckers. This will be decided by a Quebec government through laws adopted by majority vote in the National Assembly. And so from collective rights on down to the distinct society, thirst for power in some, together with apathy and sometimes stupidity in others, will have established that, as a basic element of Quebec society, a legislative majority will have the justification for arbitrarily overriding the fundamental rights of any citizen who has the privilege of living in Quebec.

XIII

THE STATE OF QUEBEC

The passages in this section were written during the dark days when Maurice Duplessis was premier of Quebec and that province enjoyed neither a proactive state nor a healthy democracy. The Quiet Revolution transformed all that, mostly for the better, so I have gladly changed the tenses from the present to the past wherever appropriate. But I haven't eliminated my explanation of our antidemocratic strains altogether, partly as a history lesson, partly as a warning. We Quebeckers still suffer too many defensive instincts against others, I'm afraid. And I worry that there is a new version of duplessisism in the fear and insularity engendered by the nationalists.

How many Quebec federalists, even among the powerful business leaders, are afraid to say publicly what they think, because their jobs, grants, or friendships might be jeopardized? Where are the politicians who went to Ottawa to fight the nationalists? Where are the intellectuals who will say, for example, that what's being taught in our history books is false? Who's fighting the lie which holds that it was the anglophone premiers and press who opposed the Meech Lake Accord, but not the francophone nationalists?

Democracy requires a respect for truth. If the books and newspapers and other media give only one version of the facts, and if the intellectuals aren't honest or courageous enough to denounce the myths and the lies, democracy inevitably will suffer. One can always say that there's nothing to be done except to despair and surrender, but one can't do politics like that. One mustn't let things slide. If one doesn't battle the purveyors of distortions and lies, things will get worse.

133

I have explained the danger implicit in regarding the state as a capricious ogre. It was this distrust that prevented French Canada in Quebec from putting the state to work for the community, in realms where individuals or groups by themselves lacked the means of acting: education, economic emancipation, social welfare, and so on.

It would not have been an unmitigated evil if only our mistaken and suspicious attitude had produced a healthy political liberalism among our fellow-citizens. The state would certainly not have intervened to serve the community; but neither would it have intervened to bully individuals and terrorize groups.

Nothing of this kind happened, and fear was firmly established among us. With that unfailing flair that seems to lead our people from one political abomination to another, we freely chose the worst of both worlds: we did nothing to make the state serve us, but we succeeded admirably in helping it enslave us.

134

A conquered people therefore not only faced a state which they feared as the creature of a foreign *nation*, but also belonged to a church which distrusted that state as a rival power and as a child of the Revolution, liable to be contaminated by anti-clericals, Protestants, or even socialists. The resulting popular attitude was a combination of political superstition and social conservatism, wherein the state – any state – was regarded as an ominous being whose uncontrollable caprices were just as likely to lead it to crush families and devour crucifixes as to help the needy and maintain order.

135

Whether or not the Conquest was the cause of all our woes, whether or not "les Anglais" were the most perfidious occupying power in the history of mankind, it was still true that the French-Canadian community held in its hands *hic et nunc* the essential instruments of its regeneration: by means of the Canadian Constitution, the Quebec state could exercise far-reaching power over the soul of French Canadians and over the territory which they occupied.

As a result, what seemed more pressing than discussing the responsibility of "les Autres" in our misadventures was that the community make effective use of the power and resources placed at its disposal by the Act of 1867. Because the community was not doing that.

136

We grew up, and our fathers before us, and their fathers before them, under a provincial state whose policy consisted in disposing of our best and most accessible natural resources, and abdicating any jurisdiction over the social organization and intellectual direction taken by French Canadians. This policy was not imposed by "les Anglais" (that is, all those who did not belong to our ethnic group), although they figured out how to exploit it to the hilt; this policy was imposed on us by our clerical and bourgeois élites: these élites have always prevented the spread of the idea that the state's role was to intervene actively in the historical process and to direct positively the community's energies towards the common weal.

137

These élites gave a succession of the most varied names to their antidemocratic spirit: the struggle against liberalism, against modernism, against freemasonry, against socialism. But whatever the case, they were acting only to protect class and caste interests against a civil authority whose exclusive responsibility should have been the public interest. Obviously, I do not mean to say that priests and the bourgeoisie claimed to be seeking anything other than the common weal; but they believed they were the only ones able to come up with a definition of that weal, and as a result they wanted neither a democratic state that would have some real existence beyond themselves, nor politicians who would exercise any authority that conflicted with their own.

138

As great as the external attack on our rights may have been, still greater was our own incapacity to exercise those rights. For example, the contempt shown by "les Anglais" for the French language never seemed to rival in extent or in stupidity that very contempt shown by our own people in speaking and teaching French in such an abominable way. Or again, the violations of educational rights of French Canadians in other provinces never seemed as blameworthy or odious as the narrow-mindedness, incompetence, and lack of foresight that have always characterized education policy in the province of Quebec. The same could be said for areas where we claimed we were being wronged: religion, finance, elections, officialdom, and so forth.

139

The Anglo-Canadians had been strong by virtue only of our weakness. This was true not only at Ottawa, but even at Quebec, a veritable charnel-house where half our rights were wasted by decay and decrepitude and the rest devoured by the maggots of political cynicism and the pestilence of corruption. Under the circumstances, can there be any wonder that Anglo-

Canadians did not want the face of this country to bear any French features? And why would they have wanted to learn a language that we had been at such pains to reduce to mediocrity at all levels of our educational system?

140

During several generations, the stability of the Canadian consensus was due to Quebec's inability to do anything about it. Ottawa took advantage of Quebec's backwardness to centralize; and because of its backwardness that province was unable to participate adequately in the benefits of centralization. The vicious circle could only be broken if Quebec managed to become a modern society. But how could this be done? The very ideology which was marshalled to preserve Quebec's integrity, French-Canadian *nationalism*, was setting up defence mechanisms the effect of which was to turn Quebec resolutely inward and backwards.

141

It befell the generation of French Canadians who came of age during the Second World War to break out of the dilemma; instead of bucking the rising tides of industrialization and modernization in a vain effort to preserve traditional values, they threw the floodgates open to forces of change. And if ever proof be required that *nationalism* is a sterile force, let it be considered that fifteen years of systematic non-*nationalism* and sometimes ruthless anti-*nationalism* at a few key points of the society were enough to help Quebec to pass from a feudal into an modern era.

142

When in Europe the dynasties and traditions had been toppled, the new societies quickly found a new cohesive agent in *nationalism*; and no sooner had privilege within the *nation* given way to internal equality than privilege between *nations* fell under attack; external equality was pursued by way of *national* self-determination. In Quebec today the same forces are at work: a new and modern society is being glued together by *nationalism*, it is discovering its potentialities as a *nation*, and is demanding equality with all other *nations*. This in turn is causing a backlash in other provinces, and Canada suddenly finds herself wondering whether she has a future.

XIV

ON NATIONALISM

Remember what Humpty Dumpty said to Alice when she was in Wonderland: words mean what you choose them to mean.

Nationalism comes from "nation," and "nation" has two distinct meanings. In the sociological sense, it means an ethnic group, a tribal group, a linguistic group, in the way we talk about the Huron nation *or the French-Canadian* nation. *(I have italicized it and its related words throughout this book whenever I'm referring to this particular meaning.) But, in the political sense, "nation" refers to a particular country or to all the people – whatever their language or ethnicity – who live within its boundaries. That's what we mean when we speak of the United Nations or the Swiss nation.*

My objection has always been to identifying a nation *in the sociological sense with a nation in the political sense. The state must govern for the good of all the people within its boundaries. If you want to call that nationalism, so be it, though I prefer to call it patriotism or the common good.*

In some situations, obviously, the two are intermingled. Suppose that Quebec became independent: as

an independent state it could take some economic mea-
sures for the good of that state. But if, within the state,
it started favouring the French over the English or any
other ethnic group, then it would be sliding from "patri-
otic" nationalism to ethnic nationalism. *I've always*
believed that a state was better if it included many
ethnic groups and governed for them all, not as groups
but as individuals. That was the basis for my belief in
federalism and why the Charter of Rights insisted on
the equality of individuals.

143

There are several potential conflicts between liberalism and the nationalist impulse. One is that liberals
are incurable internationalists – or, more precisely,
universalists – about freedom of expression and communication. Another is that nationalism is rooted in
the state, in the collectivity; while liberalism is rooted
in the person, in the individual. Hence, to avoid the
strident and chauvinistic, the narrow and defensive, the liberal will strengthen the sense of nationhood primarily by encouraging the growth of the
national individual, and of the industries and cultural institutions through which he most effectively
expresses himself.

144

The liberal's concern with freedom of the individual
must also be a concern for the milieus in which individuals develop towards their full potential.

145

In a commendable attempt to change economic facts, the state must never use legal or moral violence against its citizens. A sound economic policy must never be based on the assumption, for example, that workers would be ready to accept a drastic lowering of standards of living for the mere pleasure of seeing a national middle class replacing a foreign one at the helm of various enterprises.

As far back as my studies in Paris after the war, I learned about the theory of economic domination, which is something like the theory of monopolistic competition applied to countries. If one country is very strong in economic terms, it can call the political and economic shots on its neighbours. Therefore, I was conscious from the moment I got into politics that Canada wasn't economically independent from the United States – and couldn't be. Nor was I ever much of an economic nationalist, because I believed that the whole device of protectionism is an impoverishing one. It should only be used sparingly in areas where you can't defend your-self otherwise.

I saw that as somewhat inevitable. It's just nonsense to think that, as a large land mass with a rather small population next to the most powerful nation in the world, we could protect the whole economy. We just had to be as competitive as possible and try to balance the benefits of jobs and technology against the disadvantages of U.S. competition. Our government did nevertheless insulate certain areas from foreign ownership, such as

banking and broadcasting. We preferred to negotiate
sectoral agreements, such as Canada had with the auto
pact, rather than open the market to everything and risk
giving ourselves to the United States. And, because of
my sense of countervailing powers, we tried to build
other bridges than the ones we had to the United States
through what was called the Third Option.

146

Nationhood being little more than a state of mind,
and even sociologically distinct groups within the
nation having a contingent right of secession, the will
of the people is in constant danger of dividing up –
unless it is transformed into a lasting consensus.

The formation of such a consensus is a mysteri-
ous process which takes in many elements, such as
language, communication, association, geographi-
cal proximity, tribal origins, common interests and
history, external pressures, and even foreign intervention, none of which, however, is a determinant by
itself. A consensus can be said to exist when no
group within the nation feels that its vital interests
and particular characteristics could be better preserved by withdrawing from the nation than by
remaining within.

147

A (modern) state needs to develop and preserve this
consensus as its very life. It must continually persuade the generality of the people that it is in their
best interest to continue as a state. And since it is

physically and intellectually difficult to persuade continually through reason alone, the state is tempted to reach out for whatever emotional support it can find. Ever since history fell under the ideological shadow of the *nation*-state, the most convenient support has obviously been the idea of *nationalism*. It becomes morally "right," a matter of "dignity and honour," to preserve the integrity of the nation. Hence, from the emotional appeal called *nationalism* is derived a psychological inclination to obey the constitution of the state.

148

To say that the state uses *nationalism* to preserve its identity is not to say that the state is the inventor of *nationalism*. The feeling called *nationalism* is secreted by the nation *or nation* (in whatever sense we use the word) in much the same way as the family engenders family ties, and the clan generates clannishness. And just like clannishness, tribalism, and even feudalism, *nationalism* will probably fade away by itself at whatever time in history the *nation* has outworn its utility; that is to say, when the particular values protected by the idea of *nation* are no longer counted as important, or when those values no longer need to be embodied in a *nation* to survive.

But that time is not yet; we have not yet emerged from the era of the *nation*-state when it seemed perfectly normal for the state to rely heavily, for the preservation of the national consensus, on the gum called *nationalism*, a natural secretion of the *nation*.

In so doing, the state (or the political agents who desired a state) transformed the feeling into a political doctrine or principle of government.

149

The tiny portion of history marked by the emergence of the *nation*-states is also the scene of the most devastating wars, the worst atrocities, and the most degrading collective hatred the world has ever seen.

150

I know very well that the *nation*-state idea is not the sole cause of all the evils born of war; modern technology has a good deal to answer for on that score! But the important thing is that the *nation*-state idea has caused wars to become more and more total over the last two centuries; and that is the idea I take issue with so vehemently. Besides, each time a state has taken an exclusive and intolerant idea as its cornerstone (religion, *nationhood*, ideology), this idea has been the very mainspring of war.

151

It is not the concept of *nation* that is retrograde; it is the idea that the *nation* must necessarily be sovereign.

152

The very idea of the *nation*-state is absurd. To insist that a particular *nationality* must have complete sovereign power is to pursue a self-destructive end. Because every *national* minority will find, at the very moment of liberation, a new minority within its bosom which in turn must be allowed the right to demand its freedom. And on and on would stretch the train of revolutions, until the last-born of *nation*-states turned to violence to put an end to the very principle that gave it birth. That is why the principle of *nationality* has brought to the world two centuries of war, and *not one single* definitive solution.

Only a very, very few of the 170 or so countries of the world are homogeneous in their ethnic composition. Japan has its Korean minority; France has its Basques and Algerians; Britain has its Scots, Welsh, and Irish. If we were to follow the ethnic principle of nationality, *there would be as many countries as there are ethnic groups – which probably reach into the several thousands – to say nothing of different languages, different religions, and all the different permutations. So the modern state is a pluralistic society whose citizens must come together on the basis of their citizenship, as individuals with equal rights and mutual tolerance, not on the basis of their ethnicity or background or religion. Otherwise, it's a self-defeating principle.*

153

Now there is something for Quebec's separatists to sink their teeth into: if there is any validity to their principles they should carry them to the point of claiming part of Ontario, New Brunswick, Labrador, and New England; on the other hand, though, they would have to relinquish certain border regions around Pontiac and Temiskaming and turn Westmount into the Danzig of the New World.

I recorded that observation in 1962, more than thirty years before the movement by certain anglophone and native communities to partition themselves from Quebec in the event of its separation from Canada. I'm not claiming any prophetic powers. Logic made it absolutely predictable.

154

Nationalism, as an emotional stimulus directed at an entire community, can indeed let loose unforeseen powers. History is full of this, called variously chauvinism, racism, jingoism, and all manner of crusades, where right reasoning and thought are reduced to rudimentary proportions. It could be that in certain historical situations, where oppression was intolerable, misery unspeakable, and all alternative escape routes blocked, it was *nationalism* that sparked the subsequent break for freedom. But the arousing of such a passion as a last resort has always had its drawbacks, and the bad has invariably gone hand in hand with the good. This bad has almost always included a certain amount of despotism, because people who win their freedom with passion rather than with reason are generally disappointed to find themselves just as poor and deprived as ever; and strong governments are necessary to put an end to their unrest.

155

The *nationalists* – even those of the left – are politically reactionary because, in attaching such importance to the idea of *nation*, they are surely led to a definition of the common good as a function of an ethnic group, rather than of all the people, regardless of characteristics. That is why a *nationalistic* movement is by nature intolerant, discriminatory, and when all is said and done, totalitarian. A truly democratic government cannot be "*nationalist*," because it must pursue the good of all its citizens, without prejudice to ethnic origin. The democratic government, then, stands for and encourages good citizenship, never *nationalism*. Certainly, such a government will make laws by which ethnic groups will benefit, and the majority group will benefit proportionately to its number; but that follows naturally from the principle of equality for all, not from any right due the strongest.

156

It is possible that *nationalism* may still have a role to play in backward societies where the status quo is upheld by irrational and brutal forces; in such circumstances, *because there is no other way*, perhaps the *nationalist* passions will still be found useful to unleash revolutions, upset colonialism, and lay the foundations of welfare states; in such cases, the undesirable consequences will have to be accepted along with the good.

But in the advanced societies, where the inter-play of social forces can be regulated by law, where the centres of power can be made responsible to the people, where the economic victories are a function of education and automation, where cultural differentiation is submitted to ruthless competition, and where the road to progress lies in the direction of international integration, *nationalism* will have to be discarded as a rustic and clumsy tool.

157

Thus there is some hope that in advanced societies, the glue of *nationalism* will become as obsolete as the divine right of kings; the title of the state to govern and the extent of its authority will be conditional upon rational justification; a people's consensus based on reason will supply the cohesive force that societies require; and politics both within and without the state will follow a much more functional approach to the problems of government. If politicians must bring emotions into the act, let them get emotional about functionalism!

158

No doubt, at the level of individual action, emotions and dreams will still play a part; even in modern man, superstition remains a powerful motivation. But magic, no less than totems and taboos, has long since ceased to play an important role in the normal governing of states. And likewise, *nationalism* will eventually have to be rejected as a principle of sound government. In the world of tomorrow, the expression "banana republic" will not refer to independent fruit-growing nations but to countries where formal independence has been given priority over the cybernetic revolution. In such a world, the state – if it is not to be outdistanced by its rivals – will need political instruments which are sharper, stronger, and more finely controlled than anything based on mere emotionalism: such tools will be made up of advanced technology and scientific investigation, as applied to the fields of law, economics, social psychology, international affairs, and other areas of human relations; in short, if not a pure product of reason, the political tools of the future will be designed and appraised by more rational standards than anything we are currently using in Canada today.

XV

ON QUEBEC NATIONALISM

I have always made a distinction between nationalism in the sense of being proud of your nation and nationalism as an exclusive idea. That's why I have always objected whenever Quebec is described as the home of the French-Canadian nation. The French-Canadian nation, in a linguistic and ethnic sense, has certainly spread to other parts of Canada. The province of Quebec can hardly claim to speak for those French Canadians living beyond its borders. At the same time, Quebec is not a nation. It's a multinational entity whose government should govern for the good of every citizen, not just one linguistic group or religious group.

I was delighted by the Quiet Revolution. Jean Lesage and his Liberals did a lot of progressive things in terms of reforming the election laws, the education system, and so on. But when they began talking about "maîtres chez nous," I sensed the return of nationalism under a new guise. It wasn't the same nationalism as Duplessis's, but I felt it was a mistaken direction nevertheless. There was so much to do in terms of improving our schools and health system that I thought there wasn't any need to emphasize the fact that we weren't masters in our own house. I always believed that we would become our own masters the day we decided to educate our young people and develop our talents in business or engineering rather than concentrating on law, medicine, and the priesthood.

Nationalism is an emotional tool. It was being used to say that we French Canadians had been exploited economically in Quebec and therefore we had to build ourselves up as a nation. In my view, we had to build up this province within Confederation, by running it properly, not just for French Canadians but for every citizen of Quebec. Sure, we had had a raw deal over the centuries, but we had to look forward and pull ourselves up.

At the same time, we had to get over the siege mentality, to expand rather than close in. If we were smart, we could begin to pull our weight in Ottawa, not only in justice and public works, but in finance, foreign affairs, trade and commerce. I believed that if we were given a level playing field, we could compete as well as anyone else.

I was teaching constitutional law in the Lesage years, and I could feel the strength of the emotion in my students. Many of them were already separatists. The best and brightest were going to Quebec City, where all the action seemed to be. Meanwhile, the French Canadians in Ottawa were getting politically slaughtered by various real or imagined scandals, and we were losing whatever ground we had gained under Louis St. Laurent. I sensed the need for a counterforce. In order to prevent Quebec from getting obsessed with exercising all the power itself, there had to be some Quebeckers in Ottawa exercising some of the powers in a way that was acceptable and beneficial to French Quebeckers. It was time, I felt, to try to go to Ottawa with renewed strength.

Considering the crisis Canada was in when I became prime minister, my first priority was to reassure French-speaking Canadians that Canada was their home, not just Quebec. To do that, we had to stop making inch-by-inch progress, putting French on coins or old-age pension cheques. If Canada was their home, French Canadians had to be able to deal with their federal government in their own language wherever they went. And wherever they went, if there were enough of them, they should have the right to send their children to French classes. I gave that important assignment to my close friend and colleague Gérard Pelletier.

Our government also worked to foster the growth of an entrepreneurial class in Quebec. The first initiative was made through its Crown corporations. We made efforts to establish a base for the transportation industry in Montreal. We named French Canadians to head Air Canada, the CNR, and the communications networks. Second, we alerted our ministers and bureaucrats to the presence of excellent entrepreneurs in Quebec, in order to steer some federal contracts their way. Those French-speaking businesses would have to be as good as their English-speaking counterparts to get a bid for an open contract, but whenever we had some discretion, we tried to give them a boost. That *may have reflected a bit of prejudice on our part, but Quebec was still a "have-not" province in terms of the Canadian average.*

At some point we will have to get out of the uncertainty caused by the threat of separation. That's why we live in a social order, that's why we have laws, so that there can be some level of certitude. We know that if we sign a contract and make an agreement, this contract and agreement will be respected, perhaps not for eternity, but at least for the foreseeable future. Quebeckers simply can't go on demanding federalism and separation, independence and association, at the same time. We will have to make a clear decision based on a clear choice.

159

A people which had been defeated, occupied, decapitated, pushed out of commerce, driven from the cities, reduced little by little to a minority, and diminished in influence in a country which it had nonetheless discovered, explored, and colonized, could adopt few attitudes that would enable it to preserve its identity. This people devised a system of security, which became overdeveloped; as a result, it sometimes overvalued all those things that set it apart from others, and showed hostility to all change (even progress) coming from without.

That is why our *nationalism*, to oppose a surrounding world that was English-speaking, Protestant, democratic, materialistic, commercial, and later industrial, created a system of defence which put a premium on all the contrary forces: the French language, Catholicism, authoritarianism, idealism, rural life, and, later, the return to the land.

160

Nationalism seemed like a form of alienation, since it misdirected into hostility and vindication the very intellectual and physical energy we needed for our *national* restoration; it misdirected into struggles against "les Autres" the very forces that were needed a thousand times over to stand up to the people ultimately responsible for our own utter poverty: our so-called élites.

And among *nationalists*, the separatist faction seemed to push this alienation to absurd heights: they were ready to call to the barricades and to civil war a people who had not learned how to use constitutional weapons with courage and clearheadedness; the proof of which was the uninterrupted mediocrity of our representatives in Ottawa. The separatists called on the people for acts of heroism (since the economic and cultural "liberation" of "la Laurentie" would have greatly weakened our material and intellectual standard of living) – on the very people who did not even have the courage to stop reading American comics or to go see French movies. And with a criminal insouciance, the separatists wanted to close the borders, inevitably handing back full sovereign powers to the very élites who were responsible for the abject condition from which separatists were boldly offering to free us.

161

I would have become a French Canadian by adoption had I not been one by birth. And had French Canadians needed someone to preach collective pride to them, no doubt I would have been first on the soapbox. But good God! that is all we've had, sermons on pride and divine missions! We possessed a wealth of immense syntheses and elaborate superstructures; we went overboard on constitutional or judicial reforms, the most obvious merit of which was their lack of contact with reality.

162

Anyone whose thinking went beyond the limits of official *nationalism* or who tried to reshape it by changing a basic trait was automatically suspect: on all sides, he and his ideas were scrutinized. If he renounced *nationalism*, he was discredited and ignored; if he embraced it, his ideas were emasculated, then assimilated.

163

Alas, the *nationalists* have been harmed by their very idealism. They loved not wisely but too well, and in their desire to obtain only the best for the French Canadians, they formulated a system of social thought which could not be realized and which, for all practical purposes, left the people without any effective intellectual guidelines.

164

Clergymen, journalists, lawyers, and accountants vainly tried to become sociologists and economists, but they could not free themselves from a social environment that was traditionalist, anti-modern, and imbued with authoritarianism and fuzzy thinking.

When, accordingly, they had diagnosed our intellectual, social, and economic plight with some vigour; had censured our people's lack of spirit and exhorted them to show initiative and perseverance; had preached the familial, rural, and *national* virtues; had spoken at length of reforming the educational system; had gone over time and again the ideas they clung to; then their social thinking stopped strangely short: they had not yet said anything about our absorption into the real world of the industrial revolution.

165

In other countries, the social doctrine of the Church did much to prepare the way for the democratization of peoples, the emancipation of workers, and the progress of society. In French Canada, it was invoked in support of authoritarianism and xenophobia. What is more serious still, our doctrine made it impossible for us to solve our problems. On the negative side, it rejected any solution which might succeed among our "enemies": the English, Protestants, materialists, etc. On the positive side, it was content to set up conceptual systems bearing no objective relation to reality; the application of these systems was frequently impossible.

166

One of the most tragic episodes of the Thirties was our complete confusion in the face of unemployment, combined with our unshakable opposition to any constitutional amendment that would make it possible for Ottawa to attack the problem seriously. Our economists even managed to see to it that the unemployed in Quebec obtained less relief from federal sources than those out of work in the other provinces.

167

We have expended a great deal of time and energy proclaiming the rights due our *nationality*, invoking our divine mission, trumpeting our virtues, bewailing our misfortunes, denouncing our enemies, and avowing our independence; and for all that not one of our workmen is the more skilled, nor a civil servant the more efficient, a financier the richer, a doctor the more advanced, a bishop the more learned, nor a single solitary politician the less ignorant. Now, except for a few stubborn eccentrics, there is probably not one French-Canadian intellectual who has not spent at least four hours a week over the last year discussing separatism. That makes how many thousand times two hundred hours spent just flapping our arms? And can any one of them honestly say he has heard a single argument not already expounded *ad nauseam* twenty, forty, and even sixty years ago? I am not even sure we have exorcized any of our original bogey men in sixty years.

168

It is unlikely that any *nation*-state – or for that matter any multi*national* state – however strong, could realize a complete and perfect society; economic, military, and cultural interdependence is a *sine qua non* for states of the twentieth century, to the extent that none is really self-sufficient. Treaties, trade alliances, common markets, free-trade areas, cultural and scientific agreements, all these are as indispensable for the world's states as is interchange between citizens within them; and just as each citizen must recognize the submission of his own sovereignty to the laws of the state – by which, for example, he must fulfil the contracts he makes – so the states will know no real peace and prosperity until they accept the submission of their relations with each other to a higher order. In truth, the very concept of sovereignty must be surmounted, and those who proclaim it for the *nation* of French Canada are not only reactionary, they are preposterous.

169

The separatists will sometimes argue that, once independent, Quebec could very well afford to give up part of her sovereignty on, for instance, re-entering a

Canadian confederation, because then her choice would be her own, a free one. That abstraction covers a multitude of sins! It is a serious thing to ask French Canadians to embark on several decades of privation and sacrifice, just so that they can indulge themselves in the luxury of choosing "freely" a destiny more or less identical to the one they have rejected. But the ultimate tragedy would be in not realizing that French Canada is too culturally anaemic, too economically destitute, too intellectually retarded, too spiritually paralysed, to be able to survive more than a couple of decades of stagnation, emptying herself of all her vitality into nothing but a cesspit, the mirror of her *nationalistic* vanity and "dignity."

170

If, in my opinion, the *nation* were of purely negative value, I would not be at such pains to discredit a movement that promises to lead the French-Canadian *nation* to its ruin. The *nation* is, in fact, the guardian of certain very positive qualities: a cultural heritage, common traditions, a community awareness, historical continuity, a set of mores; all of which, at this juncture in history, go to make individuals what they are.

171

The problem we must face squarely is this: without backsliding to the ridiculous and reactionary idea of *national* sovereignty, how can we protect our French-Canadian *national* qualities?

172

Under certain circumstances there exists a right of nations to self-determination. But to claim this right without taking into account the price that will have to be paid, and without clearly demonstrating that it is to the advantage of the whole nation, is nothing short of a reckless gamble. People do not exist for states; states are created to make it easier for people to attain some of their common objectives.

Therefore, those who wish to undermine or to destroy the Canadian federal system must define clearly the risks involved and demonstrate that the new judicial and political situation they want to establish would be in the general interests of our people.

According to international law, people – in both the legal and the ethnic sense – can declare independence if they are dominated by an external power or subjugated by a terrible tyranny. Neither case applies to Quebec.

173

Clearly, an economist alone cannot tell us what the future would hold for an independent Quebec. To his knowledge must be added sociology, political science, history, and, if at all possible, a gift for prophecy. Faced with such contradictory and uncertain possibilities, a man by himself may decide to take the plunge. From dignity and pride – or even in the hope of raising his own social rank – he may declare himself ready to try *national* independence, especially if he has intellectual or financial reserves to fall back on should the adventure miscarry. But this does not hold for those people who have, at best, a precarious economic security.

174

It would seem, in fact, a matter of considerable urgency for world peace and the success of the new states that the form of good government known as democratic federalism should be perfected and promoted, in the hope of solving to some extent the worldwide problems of ethnic pluralism. To this end, Canada could be called upon to serve as mentor, provided she has sense enough to conceive of her own future on a grand scale.

XVI

THE REASON BEHIND
FEDERALISM

175

In the world of today, when whole groups of so-called sovereign states are experimenting with rational forms of integration, the exercise of sovereignty will not only be divided within federal states; it will have to be further divided between the states and the communities of states. If this tendency is accentuated the very idea of *national* sovereignty will recede and, with it, the need for an emotional justification such as *nationalism*.

176

Federalism has all along been a product of reason in politics. It was born of a decision by pragmatic politicians to face facts as they are, particularly the fact of the heterogeneity of the world's population. It is an attempt to find a rational compromise between the divergent interest groups which history has thrown together; but it is a compromise based on the will of the people.

177

Federalism is by its very essence a compromise and a pact. It is a compromise in the sense that when national consensus on *all* things is not desirable or cannot readily obtain, the area of consensus is reduced in order that consensus on *some* things be reached. It is a pact or quasi-treaty in the sense that the terms of that compromise cannot be changed unilaterally. That is not to say that the terms are fixed forever; but only that in changing them, every effort must be made not to destroy the consensus on which the federated nation rests.

The federal government neither acted unilaterally nor destroyed the consensus when it patriated the Constitution and entrenched the Charter of Rights and Freedoms in 1982. True, the government of Quebec chose not to formally agree to the package. But it was a government of separatists who, despite all sorts of offers and concessions, were never interested in building a better Canada. Instead of wanting to improve the federal pact, they wanted to destroy it. So they were the ones who rejected the consensus on which it rested – not the majority of French-speaking Canadians, not the other provinces, and certainly not Ottawa.

178

Federalism was an inescapable product of an age which recognized the principle of self-determination. For on the one hand, a sense of *national* identity and singularity was bound to be generated in a great many groups of people, who would insist on their right to distinct statehood. But on the other hand, the insuperable difficulties of living alone and the practical necessity of sharing the state with neighbouring groups were in many cases such as to make distinct statehood unattractive or unattainable. For those who recognized that the first law of politics is to start from the facts rather than from historical "might-have-beens" the federal compromise thus became imperative.

179

The principle of self-determination which makes federalism necessary makes it also rather unstable. If the heavy paste of *nationalism* is relied upon to keep a unitary *nation*-state together, much more *nationalism* would appear to be required in the case of a federal *nation*-state. Yet if *nationalism* is encouraged as a rightful doctrine and noble passion, what is to prevent it from being used by some group, region, or province within the state?

180

No amount of logic can prevent such an escalation. The only way out of the dilemma is to render what is logically defensible actually undesirable. The advantages *to the minority group* of staying integrated in the whole must on balance be greater than the gain to be reaped from separating. This can easily be the case when there is no real alternative for the separatists, either because they are met with force (as in the case of the U.S. Civil War) or because they are met with laughter (as in the case of the *Bretons bretonnants*). But when there is a real alternative, it is not so easy. And the greater the advantages and possibilities of separatism, the more difficult it is to maintain an unwavering consensus within the whole state.

181

One way of offsetting the appeal of separatism is by investing tremendous amounts of time, energy, and money in nationalism, *at the federal level*. A national image must be created that will have such an appeal as to make any image of a separatist group unattractive. Resources must be diverted into such things as national flags, anthems, education, art councils, broadcasting corporations, film boards; the territory must be bound together by a network of railways, highways, airlines; the national culture and the national economy must be protected by taxes and tariffs; ownership of resources and industry by nationals must be made a matter of policy. In short, the whole of the citizenry must be made to feel that it is only within the framework of the federal state that their language, culture, institutions, sacred traditions, and standard of living can be protected from external attack and internal strife.

182

Only blind men could expect a consensus to be lasting if the national flag or the national image is merely the reflection of one part of the nation, if the sum of values to be protected is not defined so as to include the language or the cultural heritage of some very large and tightly knit minority, if the identity to be arrived at is shattered by a colour-bar. The advantage as well as the peril of federalism is that it permits the development of a regional consensus based on regional values; so federalism is ultimately bound to fail if the nationalism it cultivates is unable to generate a national image which has immensely more appeal than the regional ones.

183

This national consensus – to be lasting – must be a living thing. There is no greater pitfall for federal nations than to take the consensus for granted, as though it were reached once and for all. The compromise of federalism is generally reached under a very particular set of circumstances. As time goes by these circumstances change; the external menace recedes, the economy flourishes, mobility increases, industrialization and urbanization proceed; and also the federated groups grow, sometimes at uneven paces, their cultures mature, sometimes in divergent directions. To meet these changes, the terms of the federative pact must be altered, and this is done as smoothly as possible by administrative practice, by judicial decision, and by constitutional amendment, giving a little more regional autonomy here, a bit more centralization there, but at all times taking great care to preserve the delicate balance upon which the national consensus rests.

184

When a large cohesive minority believes it can transfer its allegiance to a neighbouring state, or make a go of total independence, it will be inclined to dissociate itself from a consensus the terms of which have been altered in its disfavour. On the other hand, such a minority may be tempted to use its bargaining strength to obtain advantages which are so costly to the majority as to reduce to naught the advantages to the latter of remaining federated. Thus, a critical point can be reached in either direction beyond which separatism takes place, or a civil war is fought.

When such a critical point has been reached or is in sight, no amount, however great, of nationalism can save the federation. Any expenditure of emotional appeal (flags, professions of faith, calls to dignity, expressions of brotherly love) at the national level will only serve to justify similar appeals at the regional level, where they are just as likely to be effective.

185

If my premises are correct, nationalism cannot provide the answer. Even if massive investments in flags, dignity, protectionism, and Canadian content of television managed to hold the country together a few more years, separatism would remain a recurrent phenomenon, and very soon again new generations of Canadians and Quebeckers would be expected to pour their intellectual energies down the drain of emotionalism. If, for instance, it is going to remain *morally wrong* for Wall Street to assume control of

Canada's economy, how will it become *morally right* for Bay Street to dominate Quebec's or – for that matter – Nova Scotia's?

186

Thus the great moment of truth arrives when it is realized that *in the last resort* the mainspring of federalism cannot be emotion but must be reason.

XVII

ON CANADIAN PATRIOTISM

The Canadian nation must be founded upon reason. If it isn't reasonable, it shouldn't exist. But if it is reasonable, it can take a variety of positive, even emotional, measures to defend itself, so long as they don't degenerate into an ethnically based or culturally specific nationalism. That's why, to avoid confusion, I like to distinguish such positive, pragmatic, nation-building devices as patriotism.

When you're talking about defending the Canadian nation against the American nation, you're obviously talking about nationalism in the political sense, about governing the Canadian people in the way they want to be governed as opposed to the way the American people want to be governed. Thus, the governments I led began to screen all foreign investments over a certain amount in order to ensure that they bring some "significant benefit" to Canada, whether better consumer prices or better technology or more jobs. I wouldn't describe that as nationalism. I'd describe it as asking the elephant not to roll over on us.

Similarly, we preserved and affirmed Canadian identity in the whole area of foreign policy: our recognition of China, our trade with Cuba, our sovereignty over Arctic waters, our extended fishing zones, our efforts on behalf of nuclear disarmament, and so on. We weren't being anti-American. We were trying, in a positive and pragmatic fashion, to protect Canadian interests case by case as a counterweight to keep our individual citizens from being overwhelmed through the destruction of the institutions through which they express themselves.

On the other hand, as used to be the situation in Canada, if you talk about Canadian nationalism *in terms of the monarchy, the Union Jack and the English language, you're really talking about ethnic* nationalism. *Indeed, Canada had practised a fair amount of discriminatory* nationalism *against French Canadians in the past. And when you have one ethnic* nationalism *practised by one ethnic group within a state, then the minority groups are bound to produce a defensive* nationalism, *which is how French-Canadian* nationalism *developed.*

It would be unfair to think there always was equality of opportunity, even within Quebec. Obviously the richest people were the English-speaking Montrealers who had helped build the country. They were powerful, and it was natural that if the owner were English, he probably wanted English-speaking foremen and so on. The French Canadians had to struggle to make a level playing field, and that was the origin of some of the lingering resentment against the English. On the whole, however, I don't think it's very fruitful to worry about the past.

When the Lesage government talked of nationalizing the power companies to form Hydro-Québec, there was a smattering of "politique de grandeur," the politics of greatness. The gesture was partly intended to show that French Canadians can run their own enterprises, that they don't need foreign capital, and so on, which touched on ethnic or linguistic nationalism. But my government didn't create Petro-Canada or the National Energy Program to benefit one particular ethnic group within Canada. It was to preserve Canadian autonomy as much as we could against the oil multinationals who were setting our energy policy from the outside. We weren't defending one ethnic group against another. We were defending the good of the whole.

187

I know a man whose school could never teach him patriotism, but who acquired that virtue when he felt in his bones the vastness of his land, and the greatness of those who founded it.

188

If politics were a purely rational business – as it would be if people were purely rational – then perhaps we would already have abolished the *nation*-state, or at least subordinated it in a world federation of nations. But the world does not work in such a fashion. We humans are suspicious of each other. We do not fully understand even our own motivations.

And we naturally feel and understand most strongly the imperatives of the people, territory, and causes with which we are most familiar.

189

We must separate once and for all the concepts of state and of *nation*, and make Canada a truly pluralistic and polyethnic society. Now in order for this to come about, the different regions within the country must be assured of a wide range of local autonomy, such that each *national* group, with an increasing background of experience in self-government, may be able to develop the body of laws and institutions essential to the fullest expression and development of their *national* characteristics. At the same time, the English Canadians, with their own *nationalism*, will have to retire gracefully to their proper place, consenting to modify their own precious image of what Canada ought to be. If they care to protect and realize their own special ethnic qualities, they should do it within this framework of regional and local autonomy rather than a pan-Canadian one.

190

French Canadians did not develop a penchant for politics in the nineteenth century because of some sudden enthusiasm for responsible government. We had one sole passion: survival. And when viewed from this perspective, universal suffrage could very well prove to be a useful instrument. Moreover, by importing the English parliamentary system one piece at a time, our secret goal was not only to use it, but also to abuse it.

191

If French Canadians made the mistake of using democracy as a tool of ethnic warfare, the English Canadians offered them the wherewithal to learn. In all cases where fundamental oppositions arose on racial lines, the French felt a stronger force (first an army and later a majority of citizens) could always be mustered against them.

192

English-speaking Canadians, rightly considering that self-government is the noblest way of regulating social relations among free men, proceeded to claim its benefits for Canada, but only after serving standing notice on the French that such benefits were not for members of a subject race.

193

We can safely assume that the men who drew up the terms of the Canadian federal compromise had heard something of the ideology of *nationalism* which had been spreading revolutions for seventy-five years. It is likely too that they knew about the Civil War in the United States, the rebellions of 1837–8 in Canada, the Annexation Manifesto, and the unsatisfactory results of double majorities. Certainly they assessed the centrifugal forces that the constitution would have to overcome if the Canadian state was to be a durable one: first, the linguistic and other cultural differences between the two major founding groups, and, secondly, the attraction of regionalisms, which were not likely to decrease in a country the size of Canada.

194

For the incorporation of these diverse aspirations the Canadian constitution is an admirable vehicle. Under the British North America Act, the jurisdiction of the federal state of Canada concerns itself with all the things that have no specific ethnic implications, but that have to do with the welfare of the entire Canadian society: foreign affairs, the broader aspects of economic stability, foreign trade, navigation, postal services, money and banking, and so on. The provinces, on the other hand, have jurisdiction over matters of a purely local and private nature and those that affect ethnic particularities: education, municipal and parochial affairs, the administration of justice, the celebration of marriage, property and civil rights, and so forth. Nevertheless, in keeping with the fact that none of the provincial borders coincides perfectly with ethnic or linguistic delineations, no provincial government is encouraged to legislate exclusively for the benefit of a particular ethnic group in such a way as to foster a *nation*-state mentality at the provincial level.

195

The authors of the Canadian federation arrived at as wise a compromise and drew up as sensible a constitution as any group of men anywhere could have done. Reading that document today, one is struck by its absence of principles, ideals, or other frills; even the regional safeguards and minority guarantees are pragmatically presented, here and there, rather than proclaimed as a thrilling bill of rights. It has been said that the binding force of the United States of America was the idea of liberty, and certainly none of the relevant constitutional documents lets us forget it. By comparison, the Canadian nation seems founded on the common sense of empirical politicians who had wanted to establish some law and order over a disjointed half-continent. If reason be the governing virtue of federalism, it would seem that Canada got off to a good start.

196

The Fathers of Confederation showed great wisdom. Although they may have suspected that French Canadians would *in fact* always remain a linguistic minority, it seems that they wished to avoid making them feel a minority as far as *rights* were concerned. To put it another way, while recognizing that French Canadians might always feel more at home in Quebec, they attempted to prevent the law from fostering in them a sense of inferiority or from giving them any excuse to feel like aliens in other parts of Canada.

197

In substance, then, the Canadian constitution created a country where French Canadians could compete on an equal basis with English Canadians; both groups were invited to consider the whole of Canada their country and field of endeavour. Unfortunately, for reasons that on the whole reflect less credit on English than on French Canadians, the rules of the "constitutional game" were not always upheld. In matters of education, as well as political rights, the safeguards so dear to French Canadians were nearly always disregarded throughout the country, so that they came to believe themselves secure only in Quebec. Worse still, in those areas not specifically covered by the constitution, the English-speaking majority used its size and wealth to impose a set of social rules humiliating to French Canadians.

198

The rational compromise upon which the Canadian nation rested in 1867 was gradually replaced by an emotional sop; and this sop calmly assumed away the existence of one-third of the nation. In other words, the French-Canadian denizens of a Quebec ghetto, stripped of power by centralization, were expected to recognize themselves in a national image which had hardly any French traits, and were asked to have the utmost confidence in a central state where French Canada's influence was mainly measured by its not inconsiderable nuisance value.

199

Canadian *nationalism* – even after it ceased looking towards the Empire, which took quite some time – could hardly provide the basis for a lasting consensus. So time and time again, counter-*nationalist* movements arose in Quebec which quite logically argued that if Canada was to be the *nation*-state of the English-speaking Canadians, Quebec should be the *nation*-state of the French Canadians.

200

We must accept the facts of history as they are. However outworn and absurd it may be, the *nation*-state image spurred the political thinking of the British, and subsequently of Canadians of British descent in the "Dominion of Canada." Broadly speaking, this meant identifying the Canadian state with themselves to the greatest degree possible.

Since the French Canadians had the bad grace to decline assimilation, such an identification was beyond being completely realizable. So the Anglo-Canadians built themselves an illusion of it by fencing off the French Canadians in their Quebec ghetto and then nibbling at its constitutional powers and carrying them off bit by bit to Ottawa. Outside Quebec they fought, with staggering ferocity, against anything that might intrude upon that illusion: the use of French on stamps, money, cheques, in the civil service, the railroads, and the whole works.

In the face of such aggressive *nationalism*, what choice lay before the French Canadians over, say, the last century? On the one hand they could respond to the vision of an overbearing Anglo-Canadian *nation*-state with a rival vision of a French-Canadian *nation*-state; on the other hand they could scrap the very idea of *nation*-state once and for all and lead the way towards making Canada a multi*national* state.

201

The first choice was, and is, that of the separatists or advocates of independence; an emotional and prejudiced choice essentially – which goes for their antagonists too, for that matter – and I could never see any sense in it. Because either it is destined to succeed by achieving independence, which would prove that the *nationalism* of Anglo-Canadians is neither intransigent, nor armed to the teeth, nor so very dangerous for us; and in that case I wonder why we are so afraid to face these people in the bosom of a pluralistic state and why we are prepared to renounce our right to consider Canada our home *a mari usque ad mare*. Or else the attempt at independence is doomed to failure and the plight of the French Canadians will be worse than ever; not because a victorious and vindictive enemy will deport part of the population and leave the rest with dwindled rights and a ruined heritage – this eventuality seems most unlikely; but because once again French Canadians will have poured all their vital energies into a (hypothetically) fruitless struggle, energies that should have been used to match in excellence, efficacy, and persistence a (hypothetically) fearsome enemy.

The second choice, for the multi*national* state, was, and is, that of the constitutionalists. It would reject the bellicose and self-destructive idea of *nation*-state in favour of the more civilized goal of poly-ethnic pluralism.

202

In a sense the multicultural state was dreamed of by La Fontaine, realized under Cartier, perfected by Laurier, and humanized by Henri Bourassa. Anglo-Canadian *nationalism* has never enjoyed a crushing predominance and has never been in a position to refuse all compromise with the country's principal *national* minority; consequently, it has been unable to follow the policy perhaps most gratifying to its arrogance, and has had to resign itself to the situation as imposed by the course of events.

XVIII

ON BILINGUALISM

French Quebec's "state of siege" mentality was usually expressed along these lines: "We're still being attacked on all sides by the Anglos, the Protestants, the Jews, the foreigners, and anybody who goes and works with them is not to be trusted." The reason I was so happy to go to Ottawa in Jean Marchand's wake was that he was obviously a man who had spent his entire adult life working to benefit the people of Quebec. Those who thought that Quebec should separate naturally saw us as enemies and called us traitors. But I think we ended up getting so much support from Quebec because people realized we weren't traitors, we were just trying to do our best in a larger pond.

True, Ottawa in those days was very English. You could hardly speak French one minute a day. If you were writing a memo to your colleague who was equally French, you both had to communicate in English. We had the BNA Act, which said that the laws and debates in Parliament must be in both languages and so on, but in practice it was an English city. Across the river was the French city Hull but it was an industrial town dominated by the belching smokestacks of a paper mill.

As soon as we got in power, we were determined to change all that. We sent half the civil servants to Hull, we tore down the paper mill, we built a fine museum. I'm a functionalist in politics, but as rational as I try to be, I realize that people are impressed by these images. Before, when Quebec was a backward state with a largely uneducated people weak in business and the sciences, it had nowhere to go. But I knew that it would modernize someday and then it would have some place to go: it could go out of Confederation.

The enemies of bilingualism propagated the myth that everyone in Canada would have to speak French. In fact, bilingualism only meant that the federal government had to serve Canadians in both official languages. The Official Languages Act never caused anyone who wasn't bilingual to be fired. But when we started recruiting people at the bottom, we began demanding that they have a knowledge of the other language. Not everybody has an automatic right to work in the civil service of Canada. You have to have certain skills, such as reading and writing, perhaps some math and a familiarity with computers. And we said that you now have to know English and French if you want to go to the higher ranks, though not if you want to be, say, a civil servant in a post office in Moose Jaw. It was a long-term plan, and those who wanted to learn English or French were offered all kinds of costly programs.

There wasn't the same kind of backlash in Quebec about bilingualism, but there was a subtle opposition to it. The strongest argument behind the separatist and nationalist cause was that Canada was an unjust country, that Quebeckers couldn't even speak their own language in Ottawa or the courts, and so on. Well, the Official Languages Act was a terrible demolition of that argument. Never mind what happened in Manitoba in 1896; never mind what happened in Ontario before the First World War; never mind what happened in New Brunswick. Now things have changed.

At the very time we were working hard to sell the idea of two official languages in Canada, Robert Bourassa chose to make French the only official language in Quebec. If he had talked about principal language or working language, it wouldn't have done so much damage. Even so, I never considered using the power Ottawa had under the constitution to disallow his legislation. The way to change laws is to change governments, I've always believed, so it was up to the people to be better informed and their politicians more open-minded.

Despite the enormous progress the French language has made in Canada since the 1920s, you could argue that it still needs some protection from the onslaught of North American culture. But do you defend it by once again closing doors and coercing people or do you defend it by making it a matter of pride and excellence? Laws that promote the use of French, the excellence of it, the teaching of it to immigrants, are good laws, because they give people choices and opportunities to learn. That's what happened when a lot of English children began going to French immersion classes across the country because they thought of Quebec as an exciting province and French as one of the great vehicles of culture in the world. But you can hardly expect the rest of the country to respect French if English is being stamped out in Quebec.

Forcing people to do something is contrary to my nature. I believe in freedom of choice. Anyone who comes to Canada comes believing it's a free country. Yet the first thing they're told is that their kids can't go to English schools. Even René Lévesque was ashamed of it, and my government only allowed Quebec to do it under the Charter as a kind of temporary linguistic tariff, however much I disliked the spirit of it. Meanwhile, many of our own French-Canadian university students can't write proper French and can barely speak it properly. That surely isn't the fault of the British conquest or the North American environment. So why not reform the school system as a first step to make sure the language is taught properly?

At one point in history everybody was using French as the language of diplomacy, culture, science. Today English is the international language of business, technology, and so on. That's a given. If you try to fight it artificially, you'll condemn your people to a new dark age. Instead, you have to counter this reality with superiority. The Swedes, for example, aren't losing their language, despite being just a small country in Europe: they're keeping it while picking up two or three others. Similarly, I believe in promoting the French language by promoting the excellence of the people who speak it. A proud people will keep their language precisely because they're proud of it. But if you have to scare or threaten them into keeping it, you're never going to have a proud people who are determined to preserve their language and preserve it freely rather than by coercion.

There are still some people in Canada who want to turn the clock back, who say it's so much simpler to run the country with one part speaking French and the other speaking English. But you won't run a country very long that way. At some point one part will say that it doesn't need the other, that it's less expensive not to translate everything, that we might as well just separate.

203

My friends and I entered federal politics for the precise purpose of proving that French Canadians could be at home in Canada outside Quebec and could exercise their rights in the federal capital and throughout the country. This was also the purpose of the Official Languages Act and of the emergence of what the English-speaking press was soon calling "French power."

The separatists of both Quebec and the West well understood what was happening. Conscious that their ultimate goal presupposed an exclusively English-speaking Canada and an exclusively French-speaking Quebec, they abandoned their minorities in other provinces – French-speaking and English-speaking – and fought tooth and nail against the policy of bilingualism, which in their terms was the work of traitors and double-dealers.

204

As far back as memory serves, French Canadians had been essentially asking for one thing: respect for the French fact in Canada and incorporation of this fact into Canadian civil society, principally in the areas of language and education, and particularly in the federal government and provinces with French-speaking minorities. After two centuries of struggle and a few symbolic victories (bilingual money and stamps, for example), the Official Languages Act was passed in 1969 and minority-language education rights were entrenched in the Charter of 1982. The gates had suddenly opened and institutional bilingualism was recognized in Canada.

Then, equally suddenly, the Quebec *nationalists* no longer wanted the French language to be made equal with English throughout Canada. They denounced bilingualism as utopic at the very moment it was becoming a reality. With Bills 22 and 101, Quebec declared itself *unilingually* French and abandoned the cause of French-speaking minorities in other provinces, the better to marginalize the English-speaking minority in Quebec; the Quiet Revolution had suddenly empowered us to become indifferent to the first minority and intolerant of the second. It is as if we had practised virtue only out of weakness or hypocrisy.

205

The issue at stake is not the mere survival of the French language and of the cultural values relating to it. Their survival is already assured. French is spoken in Quebec by an ever-increasing number of persons. If one discounts the possibility of genocide or of some major cataclysm, it seems certain that in this part of America French will continue to be spoken regardless of what happens to the constitution.

The problem is therefore to stimulate our language and culture so that they are alive and vital, not just fossils from the past. We must realize that French will only have value to the extent that it is spoken by a progressive people. What makes for vitality and excellence in a language is the collective quality of the people speaking it. In short, the defence of the French language cannot be successful without accomplishments that make the defence worthwhile.

206

The day of language barriers is finished, at least as far as science and culture are concerned; and if Quebec's intellectuals refuse to master a language other than their own, if they will recognize no loyalty but to their *nation*, then they may be renouncing forever their place among the world's intellectual élite.

207

The French language will be able to express progressive values only if North Americans who speak it are themselves in the forefront of progress, that is to say, if they compete on an equal basis with English-speaking Canadians.

But the competition *must* be on an equal basis. Otherwise, the French population is in danger of

becoming paralysed by an excess of defensive mechanisms. We shall develop the mentality of a belea-
guered people, withdrawing into Quebec the better
to sustain the siege. In other words, French Canadians
may be forced by *English*-speaking *nationalism* to
push Quebec nearer to a *national* state and sooner or
later to independence.

208

I am afraid that excessive preoccupation with the
future of the language has made certain people forget
the future of the person speaking it. A working man
may care about his language and cultural values; he
also cares very strongly about having a decent life
without the risk of losing the little he has through
some misguided political adventure.

209

Bilingualism unites people; dualism divides them.
Bilingualism means you can speak to the other; dual-
ity means you can live in one language and the rest of
Canada will live in another language.

210

Quebec experiences the diversity of Canada where it
lives; it is part of its deepest self. If Quebec were to
deny, or to claim to lessen or neglect this vital dimen-
sion of its being, it would commit an injustice, a
betrayal of its responsibility which would result in
continuing self-impoverishment.

211

Languages have two functions. They act both as a vehicle of communication, and as a preservation of culture. Governments can support languages in either or both of these roles, but it is only in the communication role that the term "official" is employed. An overwhelming number of Canadians use either English or French in their day-to-day communications with one another and with government. It is for this practical reason – not some rationalization about races – that these two languages have attained an official character in Canada. French and English are not superior to or more precise than any other language. They are simply used more in Canada.

212

If French Canadians are able to claim equal partnership with English Canadians, and if their culture is established on a coast-to-coast basis, it is mainly because of the balance of linguistic forces within the country. Historical origins are less important than people generally think, the proof being that neither Inuit nor Indian dialects have any kind of privileged position. On the other hand, if there were six million people living in Canada whose mother tongue was Ukrainian, it is likely that this language would establish itself as forcefully as French. In terms of realpolitik, French and English are equal in Canada because each of these linguistic groups has the power to break the country.

XIX

ON MULTICULTURALISM

The first argument I had when I got to Ottawa wasn't about bilingualism, it was about multiculturalism. Bilingualism, yes, because you can work in two languages or even more. But you can't expect everybody to have only two cultures, because there are a lot more than two cultures in the country.

Bilingualism is a tool that doesn't necessarily imply you're of French or Anglo-Saxon culture. It implies that you see it as a necessary and useful step to recognize the languages of the Europeans who first settled what became Canada. Anybody who really wants to learn a language can do so. But you can't learn an entire culture. Besides, I have always believed in the superiority of the multinational society. The variety of cultures in Canada undoubtedly contributes to the country's richness and prosperity.

quote

213

National unity, if it is to mean anything in the deeply personal sense, must be founded on confidence in one's own *individual* identity; out of this can grow respect for that of others and a willingness to share ideas, attitudes, and assumptions. A vigorous policy of multiculturalism will help create this initial confidence. It can form the basis of a society which is founded on fair play for all.

214

We have concluded in Canada almost without debate that true greatness is not measured in terms of military might or economic aggrandizement. On a planet of finite size, the most desirable of all characteristics is the ability and desire to cohabit with persons of differing backgrounds, and to benefit from the opportunities which this offers.

215

The decision by the Canadian government that a second language be given increased official recognition is, in indirect fashion, support for the cultivation and use of many languages, because it is a breach of the monopoly position of one language and an elevation of the stature of languages that are "different."

216

Every single person in Canada is now a member of a minority group. Linguistically our origins are one-third English, one-third French, and one-third neither. We have no alternative but to be tolerant of one another's differences. Beyond the threshold of tolerance, however, we have countless opportunities to benefit from the richness and variety of a Canadian life which is the result of this broad mix. The fabric of Canadian society is as resilient as it is colourful. It is a multicultural society; it offers to every Canadian the opportunity to fulfil his or her own cultural instincts and to share those from other sources. This mosaic pattern, and the moderation which it includes and encourages, makes Canada a very special place.

217

Uniformity is neither desirable nor possible in a country the size of Canada. We should not even be able to agree upon the kind of Canadian to choose as a model, let alone persuade most people to emulate it. There are surely few policies potentially more disastrous for Canada than to tell all Canadians that they must be alike. There is no such thing as a model or ideal Canadian. What could be more absurd than the concept of an "all-Canadian" boy or girl? A society which emphasizes uniformity is one which creates intolerance and hate. A society which eulogizes the average citizen is one which breeds mediocrity. What the world should be seeking, and what we in Canada must continue to cherish, are not concepts of uniformity but human values: compassion, love, and understanding.

XX

THE PEOPLE'S PACKAGE

When I was minister of justice, I argued against reopening the constitution. It's a can of worms. Besides, it was working well enough, in that most of the real problems facing Canadians could be remedied under it, so why waste political time and energy fixing it needlessly? But the real push came when John Robarts, the premier of Ontario, convened the Confederation of Tomorrow conference and all the provinces came. After that, I readjusted my advice and said, Well, the can of worms is open now, and if we don't want it to be a complete mess, let's at least make sure we have our say.

Some people in Quebec have the temerity to suggest that when I promised change during the 1980 referendum campaign, I meant that we would change the constitution according to how the Yes side would have changed it, had they won. That isn't very logical. I had always fought special status. I had always fought the over-decentralization of a country that was already the most decentralized in the world. The Yes side had lost fair and square. And it's not as though we didn't bring in change. We brought in a constitution with a charter of rights.

I think I had proven my point to the Canadian people that they would never get their constitution unless they submitted to blackmail from some very greedy premiers. Therefore I proposed splitting the constitutional package into what I called the people's package (patriation with a charter of rights) and the government's package (an amending formula and some functional horse-trading as to which level of government can best deliver the services to the Canadian people). But the provinces saw that, once patriation and a charter happened, they would have no more leverage, so they objected to the proposal.

We never intended to give Ottawa the power to resolve all conflict in its favour, although that is what John A. Macdonald had wanted at first. We were simply asking that the conflicts be resolved by the constitution itself. We were asking that each province and, through a charter of rights and freedoms, each Canadian be able to claim the constitution's protection. We were asking that, when the constitution was brought home, Parliament be given one basic power: the power to seek agreement with the provinces and, if that produced deadlock, to ask the people to break the deadlock.

In doing that, I forever gave up Ottawa's chance of going it alone to London. Now it would need either some or all of the provinces to go with it. And, in the Charter, I gave them many of the fundamental changes they had asked for, including, against my fondest wishes, the notwithstanding clause. Even the constitutional amending formula wasn't ours – ours, incidentally, would have given Quebec back the veto that Robert Bourassa and René Lévesque had thrown away – but one worked out in the West and against my liking because it permitted provinces to opt out.

Some of my ministers wanted to use patriation as a way of grabbing more federal powers. I said, no, this is to be the people's package. We can take powers away from the provinces and the federal government by protecting the citizens in the Charter, but we can't shift the balance between Ottawa and the provincial governments. That would come in stage two, once we got a fair negotiating process and an amending formula.

Of course, the separatists were outraged, because they wanted to break up the country. But if you were to ask what the Quebec people themselves thought, you would have to look to their representatives in both capitals as well as to the polls. And though it's unfortunate that the Quebec government of the time didn't sign, Quebec was not "left out" as a result. It's well and truly tied to the constitution by virtue of the rules of the game laid down by the Supreme Court.

So what exactly are the nationalists complaining about? Didn't they complain that we were part of the British Empire? Well, we patriated the constitution from Great Britain. And what about the Charter? It's one of the fairest and most advanced in the world. And what about the amending formula? It was quite similar to the one accepted by René Lévesque. So why weren't the nationalists celebrating in the streets? If we hadn't proceeded at that time, we would have backed

away from patriation forever. And that's why I think
that a lot of those who now whine about how it was
done are crybabies.

218

Essentially, a constitution is designed to last a long
time. Legal authority derives entirely from it; and if
it is binding only for a short period it is not binding
at all. A citizen – to say nothing of a power group –
will not feel obliged to respect laws or governments
he considers unfavourable to him if he thinks that
they can easily be replaced; if the rules of the constitutional game are to be changed in any case, why not
right now? A country where this mentality is preva-
lent oscillates between revolution and dictatorship.

219

The constitution had very little to do with the state
of economic, technical, and demographic inferiority
in which the French Canadians of Quebec found
themselves. I was not in a frantic hurry to change the
constitution, simply because I *was* in a frantic hurry
to change reality. And I refused to give the ruling
classes the chance of postponing the solving of *real*
problems until after the constitution had been
revised. We had seen only too often how, in the past,
discussions centring on ideas such as the form of
the state, *nationhood*, provincial autonomy, and
independence served to conceal the impotence of the
ruling classes when faced with the profound transformation of our society by the industrial revolution.

All I asked of our ruling classes was that they stop being so preoccupied with the hypothetical powers an independent Quebec might have, and start using the powers the real Quebec did have a bit more often and a bit more wisely.

220

From 1927 right up to 1979, during a long series of federal–provincial conferences, all Canadian prime ministers had sought to replace the British North America Act, which served as a constitution, with an authentically Canadian constitution. Each attempt failed because one or more provinces had come out against it.

221

"Constitutional evolution" presupposed precisely that Canada would have its constitution and would be able to amend it. Almost invariably, it was the Quebec provincial government that blocked the process. Thus, in 1965, Jean Lesage and his minister at the time, René Lévesque, withdrew their support from the Fulton–Favreau formula (a plan to amend the British North America Act) after they had accepted and defended it. And Robert Bourassa, who in Victoria in 1971 had proposed a formula which gave Quebec a right of absolute veto over all constitutional amendments, withdrew his own endorsement ten days after the conference. In both cases, the reason for backing off was the same: Quebec would "permit" Canada to Canadianize the colonial document we had instead of a constitution, only if the rest of Canada granted Quebec a certain "special status."

222

In 1980 a majority of the Quebec people rejected the separatist option by answering No to a quite convoluted question (which some people could have considered contemptuous and fraudulent). The Canadian government considered that Canada had avoided disintegration and should make a supreme effort to acquire formal sovereignty, by breaking any constitutional link with Great Britain, and by acquiring a charter of human rights which applied to all Canadians.

223

During the 1980–82 constitutional exercise, the federal government proposed to cut the Gordian knot by arguing that the sovereignty of Canada ultimately resided neither in the provinces nor in the federal government, but in the Canadian people. The provincial governments collectively rejected that view, even objecting to the use of the words "the people of Canada" in a preamble to the constitution and proposing instead a description of Canada as a country made up of "provinces . . . freely united," thus returning to the self-same concept that had prevented patriation in 1927.

The premiers also unanimously made it abundantly clear, by the so-called Château Consensus, on September 12, 1980, that they would never permit the patriation of the Canadian constitution until juris-dictional power had been drastically reallocated in favour of the provinces.

224

The federal government took the position that a reallocation of powers between the two orders of government was a legitimate subject of negotiation, but that the right of Canadians to have a constitu-tion of their own should not be subordinated to the open-ended process of satisfying any premier's insa-tiable desire for increased provincial powers. Since it was generally recognized that, technically speak-ing, patriation of the constitution could proceed only from a resolution of the Parliament of Canada addressed to the Parliament at Westminster, and since such a joint address had never been moved, for lack of sufficient provincial support, it appeared that complete sovereignty for Canada – as well as the vesting of that sovereignty in the Canadian people – could forever be held to ransom by one or more provinces. Fifty-three years of failure were there to prove the point.

225

There were only two ways to solve the conundrum. The government of Canada could accept the "com-pact theory," recognizing that our country was nothing more than a community of communities, in which fundamental powers (including the power to patriate the constitution) flowed from the provinces that had freely united to form a loose confederation. Or the government of Canada, as the sole governing body empowered to act in the name of all Canadians, could reject the compact theory, hold that Canada was something more than and different from the sum of its parts, and proceed to patriate the constitution unilaterally. We chose the latter course.

226

Was this a "coup de force" or a legal political decision? We would soon find out: three provinces (Quebec among them) put the question to the Supreme Court and got a ruling in September 1981, according to which the operation would be legal, although it offended customary practice.

Everyone then returned to the negotiating table. The Gang of Eight provinces (including Quebec) made several counterproposals, which were accepted in the hopes of reaching unanimity: the "notwithstanding" clause reduced the impact of the Charter, Alberta's amending formula replaced the Victoria formula, the provinces would acquire some new jurisdictions relating to indirect taxation and international trade. In spite of all that, we were in a deadlock again.

227

At the beginning of November 1981, the federal side made a proposal which temporarily got the support of the government of Quebec, but which displeased the seven provinces in alliance with Quebec. These latter provinces felt betrayed and let it be known they would seek a compromise solution without Quebec. The compromise was found and was offered to the government of Quebec, which refused to accept it. Once more, Canada decided to declare independence without the unanimous consent of the provinces.

Was this a "coup de force" or a legal political decision? We would soon find out: Quebec put the question to the Supreme Court and was told that the operation was legal and did not breach customary practice, since no single province had a veto power. The same court ruled that Quebec was indeed bound by the Constitution Act of 1982.

228

Not surprisingly, the federal government and nine provincial governments chose to proceed, supported in that course by 71 out of the 75 members of Parliament elected from Quebec, and by 38 of the 108 deputies elected to Quebec's National Assembly, for a total weighted support of 65 per cent of all elected representatives from "la belle province."

That argument is rejected, of course, by those people who think that the Quebec government alone speaks for the Quebec people. If you hold that view, you're by definition a separatist, because if you believe in Canada, you have to recognize that the Quebec government speaks for the Quebec people in some areas, such as education and health care, while the federal government speaks for the Quebec people in other

areas, such as foreign affairs and interprovincial trade.
So, if you believe in Canada, you have to say that the
National Assembly and the Parliament of Canada
both speak for Quebec.

229

In the wake of that support came three public opinion
polls taken in Quebec during the months following
patriation, showing that the people of Quebec also
firmly agreed with the 1982 constitutional amendment. That in turn was followed by the rapid disintegration of the Parti Québécois and the concomitant
resurgence of the Quebec economy, which placed
well above the Canadian average. One might even
add that four of the five judges on the Quebec Court
of Appeals had previously legitimized the patriation
process (in April 1981).

So much for the babble that Quebeckers had felt
victimized by the sequence of events beginning with
the "No" victory in the 1980 referendum and ending
with the patriation of the constitution in 1982.

230

Once the provinces had appealed to the Supreme
Court as the arbiter of conventions, surely those
provinces had no choice but to accept that there
would be winners and losers. How then can politicians and academics argue, as they do today, that
one loser had been unfairly treated by the Fates he
himself had conjured?

Indeed, was not the unkindest fate of all the one meted out to the government of Canada, which, as a consequence of the Supreme Court decision, was faced with the choice of either patriating the constitution according to the legal and conventional rules set down by Canada's highest tribunal or backing down in front of a provincial government whose avowed purpose was nothing less than the destruction of Canada?

If we had done the latter, Canada would have ceased to be governed by the rule of law, having recognized that now and forever more the highest law in the land could only evolve and be determined through a process of political blackmail manipulated by one province.

XXI

ON SPECIAL STATUS

The whole thrust of my contributions to Cité Libre *was that French Quebeckers were obsessed by a siege mentality. As a minority, we probably were right to have defended ourselves during the nineteenth century and the beginning of the twentieth. But after the Second World War the world was becoming one world, and here we were in our fortress while the human caravan was marching on. That wasn't in keeping with our heritage and ancestors. After all, it was the French who discovered the Rockies, who went to the polar seas and down the Mississippi to the Gulf of Mexico. Yet, here we were, closing ourselves into a little Quebec rather than trying to conquer the country and the world. We were also cutting ourselves off from the very important pockets of francophones in Ontario, the West, and the Maritimes, as though we weren't equal to the task we were facing.*

The same inferiority complex persists in the notion of special status for Quebec. But if you give special powers to one province in a federal system, so that it can legislate in areas where only the central government can legislate for the rest of the country, the obvious result will be to diminish Quebec's weight in Ottawa. Suppose communications and the environment get shifted to Quebec jurisdiction, then we would be unlikely to ever again have a Quebecker as federal minister in those fields. Whatever influence we gain here, we lose there. So we have to choose. If we want to become independent and take all the powers, too bad but okay. But we can't have our cake and eat it too.

I know that the nationalists want independence, and I know that the people don't want it. So the nationalists have settled on creeping independence, étapisme. They want to take this power now, then that power, and eventually Quebeckers will feel that they govern more from Quebec than from Ottawa – and then they take the last step and do it all. The real and ultimate goal of Quebec's nationalist politicians is to undo the defeat of the Plains of Abraham. As Jacques Parizeau once admitted, if we try to kill the whole bird, Quebeckers will object, but if we take a feather here and a feather there, we'll end by unfeathering the whole bird and no one will notice.

Of course, there already are special powers for Quebec in the 1867 constitution by the mere fact that property and civil rights is a provincial responsibility and that Quebec alone has its civil code. And Quebec also has special status by Section 133, which says that French and English will be used in its legislature. So there are differences. But if you have massive and continual pressure to shift powers from Ottawa to one province, then you're creating a special status that unbalances the constitution, with the inevitable result that more and more Quebeckers in politics or the civil service will ask, Why should I go to Ottawa? Our best and brightest would stay in Quebec.

When I became prime minister, I was always try-ing to move French-speaking Canadians into posts they had never occupied in Ottawa. At one point we had a French-speaking governor general, prime minis-ter, chief of defence staff, head of the RCMP, minister of finance, and so on. We were establishing, to the delight of Quebeckers, that they could help run the country as well as anyone from Ontario or elsewhere. As for the defence of our language, we introduced the Official Languages Act and the Charter of Rights and Freedoms. That's why I think we got such massive support from Quebec. And that's why I groan when I hear calls for special status, as though we need crutches because we're not bright enough or can't protect our own lan-guage. Well, you can't have crutches against the world. You have to get out and fight.

231

The Quiet Revolution and its effects had trans-formed the province of Quebec into a modern society in which francophones were at last feeling capable of handling the political, economic, and cultural chal-lenges inherent on a predominantly English-speaking continent. In Quebec, however, the political classes seemed increasingly to be bent on emphasizing the defence of French Quebec rather than the advance-ment of *all* Quebeckers and of francophones in other provinces. Hence the infatuation of Quebec politicians with all those turns of phrase that imply a loosening of federal ties: special status, distinct society, equality or independence, sovereignty-association.

232

I have always opposed the notions of special status and distinct society. With the Quiet Revolution, Quebec became an adult and its inhabitants have no need of favours or privileges to face life's challenges and to take their rightful place within Canada and in the world at large. They should not look for their "identity" and their "distinctness" in the constitution, but rather in their confidence in themselves and in the full exercise of their rights as citizens equal to all other citizens of Canada.

233

The real question to be asked is whether the French Canadians living in Quebec need a provincial government with more powers than the other provinces.

I believe it is insulting to us to claim that we do. The new generation of business executives, scientists, writers, film-makers, and artists of every description has no use for the siege mentality in which the élites of bygone days used to cower. The members of this new generation know that the true opportunities of the future extend beyond the boundaries of Quebec, indeed beyond the boundaries of Canada itself. They don't suffer from any inferiority complex, and they say good riddance to the times when we didn't dare to measure ourselves against "others" without fear and trembling. In short, they need no crutches.

Quite the contrary, they know that Quebeckers are capable of playing a leading role within Canada and that – if we wish it – the entire country can provide us with a powerful springboard. In this, today's leaders have finally caught up with the rest of the population, which never paid much heed to inward-looking *nationalism* – that escape from reality in which only the privileged could afford to indulge.

234

All the various kinds of "special status" which have been discussed until now, whatever their content, lead to the following logical problem: how can a constitution be devised to give Quebec greater powers than other provinces, without reducing Quebec's power in Ottawa? How can citizens of other provinces be made to accept the fact that they would have less power over Quebec at the federal level than Quebec would have over them? How, for example, can Quebec assume powers in foreign affairs, which other provinces do not have, without accepting a reduction of its influence in the field of foreign affairs through the federal government? How can Quebec be made the *national* state of French Canadians, with really *special* powers, without abandoning at the same time demands for the parity of French and English in Ottawa and throughout the rest of the country?

These questions remain unanswered, because they are unanswerable. For to think about them is to realize that we must have the courage and lucidity to make a choice.

235

That Quebec is a distinct society is totally obvious. The inhabitants of the province live in a territory defined by its borders. The majority speak French. They are governed under a particular set of laws. And these realities have been pivotal in the development of a culture which is uniquely theirs.

These are inarguable facts, arising from two centuries of history marked by intense struggles and juridico-political stubbornness. This produced the Canadian Constitution of 1867, whose federative rather than unitary form was imposed by French Canadians, led by Sir George-Étienne Cartier, on other Canadians. It was precisely this federalism which enabled and encouraged the development in Quebec of a province that is a distinct society.

This constitution also gave birth to nine other provinces, all of them distinct from the others by reason of their territorial borders, their ethnic composition, their laws, and hence their cultures. (A society cannot be distinct in relation to another, in fact, without that other being distinct in relation to the first.) Nonetheless, all these distinct societies share a considerable heritage, despite misconceptions to the contrary.

It is a truism if not a platitude to assert that Quebec is a distinct society, since the constitution we adopted in 1867 has permitted it to be a distinct society. Since this is constitutionally recognized already, why are so many Quebec politicians, public law experts, and business people clamouring to have it inserted in the constitution all over again? And why do they say they are humiliated when people wonder why this is so necessary?

Because, they say, the Constitution of 1982 recognizes the collective rights of other communities: ancestral rights of the native peoples, the multicultural heritage of many newer Canadians, even women's rights. So why such niggardliness when it comes to writing into the same constitution "the promotion of Quebec as a distinct society"?

This is gross sophistry. Unlike Quebeckers, neither the native peoples nor the "multiculturals" nor women are collectivities defined by a specific territory and enjoying executive, legislative, and juridical powers. Consequently, the constitution does not give them, as collectivities, any specific jurisdictional power to "promote" their distinct societies. The only effect of these Charter provisions is to give individuals belonging to these collectivities an additional guarantee of protection against any interpretation of the Charter whereby their rights could be overlooked. Somewhat in the same fashion, the Charter has given to members of the French-Canadian collectivity scattered throughout Canada not the power to make laws to promote the French language, but the power to have the courts insist on the equality of French with English, to the extent guaranteed by the Charter.

237

Now the consequences of "distinct society" become clear. The Charter, whose essential purpose was to recognize the fundamental and inalienable rights of all Canadians equally, would recognize thenceforth that in the province of Quebec these rights could be overridden or modified by provincial laws whose purpose would be to promote a distinct society and more specifically to favour "the French-speaking majority" that has "a unique culture" and "a civil law tradition." There is a very good chance, then, that Quebeckers of Irish, Jewish, or Vietnamese origin – even if they speak French – would have trouble claiming to belong to this "distinct society" in any attempt to protect their fundamental rights as individuals against discriminatory laws enacted in a jurisdiction where they are in a minority. And even an "old stock" Quebecker would risk losing his fundamental rights if he were rash enough to pit them against Quebec laws passed for the promotion of "collective rights."

—

238

Every time a new demand is announced, the self-appointed élites snap to attention, ready to feel humiliated if the ransom is not paid at once. Most incredible of all, there are still good souls in English Canada who are ready to take these temper tantrums seriously and urge their compatriots to pay each new ransom for fearing of losing each "last chance" to save Canada. Poor things, they have not yet realized that the *nationalists'* thirst will never be satisfied, and that each new ransom paid to stave off the threat of schism will simply encourage the master blackmailers to renew the threat and double the ransom.

239

All the demands made of Canada by the Quebec *nationalists* can be summed up in just one: keep giving us new powers and the money to exercise them, or we'll leave. If Quebeckers are offered the chance to have their cake and eat it too, naturally they will accept. But as Canadians they also know that a country must choose to be or not to be; that dismantling Canada will not save it, and the *nationalists* cannot be allowed to play the game of heads-I-win-tails-you-lose, or to hold referendums on independence every ten years. And anyway, you cannot *really* believe in Canada and at the same time claim the right of self-determination for Canadian provinces.

—

166

If you could say, well, we'll recognize one or two aspects where Quebec will have different powers than the rest of the provinces and that will be that, I might go along with it kicking and screaming. But the dynamic of national-ist *politics is always to ask for more. The* nationalists *who are separatists are doing it deliberately in order to get more power for themselves and destabilize the federation. The nationalists who aren't separatists are doing it without understanding the destructive consequences of open-ended, one-way demands.*

That's one reason why I found the Meech Lake Accord so unacceptable. The Mulroney government was ready to cede to the provinces all sorts of matters, but Ottawa asked for nothing in return. Furthermore, the Accord was just the first step after which the Quebec government was going to demand more and more. Premier Bourassa created the Allaire Commission to do precisely that even while the Meech Lake Accord was still being discussed by the provinces. So those who thought that it was about to bring "peace in our time" were dreaming in Technicolor.

240

For unscrupulous politicians, there is no surer way of rousing feelings than to trumpet a call to pride of race. French Canadians will be rid of this kind of politician if the blackmail ceases, and the blackmail will cease only if Canada refuses to dance to that tune.

XXII

ON DECENTRALIZATION

I believe in balance. Too much state interference is bad; too little is bad. Too much provincial power is bad; too little is bad. You have to look for counterweights all the time. When I first went to Ottawa as a civil servant, I returned thinking that we had to give more powers to the provinces, because Ottawa was doing everything. Meanwhile, even the enlightened part of the population was saying that if Quebec couldn't solve the problem of its universities, Ottawa should give money to them. I said that we had to build up our own government in Quebec, which is what happened when the Quiet Revolution took place.

Some things just bring emotional reactions, such as "decentralization is good for democracy" or "centralization is bad for the country." My position has always been, let's put the powers where they function best. If health care and education can be well delivered by the provinces, let's leave them where the Constitution has them. But if we're talking about aeronautics or the environment, it's hard to see how they could be regulated by one city or province, so perhaps they should come under federal jurisdiction.

I was trying to take the passion out of politics at a time when people were arguing for separation or more provincial rights or the compact theory. When some people wanted to change the monarchy, either to strengthen it or abolish it, I'd say, why fix it if it isn't broken? It may not be all that useful, but changing it would have involved a great deal of emotion and political capital, so why bother? And that was my approach when the Lesage government wanted to nationalize the power companies. They could be improved, no doubt, but the money it cost to nationalize them could have been better spent on education. Mine was a functional, common-sense approach.

Every premier in every provincial government is elected by the people to stick up for the interests of their province. When the premier of Quebec gets a shipping contract, and the premier of Alberta fights for better oil prices, they are just doing their jobs. But the government of Canada is elected to seek the good of the whole country, and sometimes it will have to say no to one region in order to redistribute revenues or equality of opportunity. In other words, the federal system uses counterweights, which means there is always some tension – creative tension, I hope, but tension nonetheless.

I never objected to that tension. I did object when a premier tried to get more power for his province in order to help a particular ethnic group. The duty of a premier is to fight for the good of all the people in that province, not just one ethnic group, even if it happens to be the majority. And I objected when Quebec, more

169

often than not, said it wanted more powers, more money, more special status, or else it would leave the federation. I'm a Canadian and a Quebecker, and I think we have a great country and that it's everybody's job to try to make it greater. I don't like those who use blackmail and threaten to get out if they don't feel loved enough.

While the premiers were fighting for the good of their provinces, I had to fight for the good of the country. When it was simply a conflict of interest, we often solved it by negotiation – but not when it involved a conflicting vision of Canada. For there was a view that Canada only exists courtesy of the provinces, that it's the servant of the provinces. That tended to weaken the national identity, in my view, and I fought it just as Macdonald and Laurier had fought it. The people of Canada had to decide on their view of the country: Is it a nation greater than the sum of its parts or is it a confederation of shopping centres?

The National Energy Program, for example, was a conflict between the greater good of a region and the greater Canadian good. The premier of Alberta wasn't fighting for the benefit of any particular ethnic group, but he was fighting for his region against the federal government. That's always the problem of a federal state, because there were always inequalities between the various regions, and it is the job of the central government to think of the whole. In other words, federal ministers and MPs have to put aside where they come from and become Canadian patriots vis-à-vis the regionalists in somewhat the same way they are

Canadian patriots when trying to defend their country against the overpowering economic domination of the United States.

Ironically, I began as a defender of the provinces. My very first article in Cité Libre was about the great degree of centralization that had occurred before and during the Second World War. But it seemed obvious that, as the emerging social forces kept calling for more state intervention in education, social services, and other provincial areas, there would be a natural move back towards decentralization through the operation of the constitution. If the provinces try to get more powers, I argued, Ottawa would try to get more powers too, but if we just let the thing operate as it is, the provinces will become enormously more important – which they did. And I thought, given how the constitution was structured and the way society was evolving, there was nothing wrong with more and more powers being exercised by the provinces, provided they didn't go beyond a certain point. In fact, by the time I left office, the federal government was taking less than 40 per cent of the tax revenues.

Remember, too, that it was the government of Quebec and the government of Montreal that spoke of apprehended insurrection in October 1970 and wrote to Ottawa, pleading for us to bring in the War Measures Act. According to the logic of some critics, we should have said no. But in the name of what? Centralism or provincial autonomy? Would we have had Quebec's support if we hadn't accepted what they said was necessary? Should we not have listened to the government of

Quebec when it was asking for something that it deemed necessary for the administration of justice?

But, as the 1970s developed, with one constitutional conference after another, I realized that nothing could satisfy the appetite of the provinces. Once the Parti Québécois began attending those meetings, its tactics began to impress the other provincial governments. Until then Quebec had been the only one that had seriously asked for many more powers from the federal government. Until then the game had been about more money. Now the other premiers began saying, We need much more to do our job, to be close to the people, to serve them well. It was soon obvious that we were no longer just fighting separatism. We were fighting the rebirth of the theory that Canada is the creation of the provinces rather than the creation of the sovereign Canadian people. Everything was up for grabs. The list of the powers the provinces wanted grew longer and longer, until I reached a point where I thought we had decentralized enough.

Whenever a provincial government has some particular argument or quarrel with the federal government, it fights tooth and nail to win its point. It's perfectly justified in doing so, just as the federal government is justified in trying to assert the national interest. But, whenever we had these kinds of discussions with a provincial government or at a federal–provincial conference, the opposition parties in Ottawa usually took the side of the provincial governments. My quarrel with them wasn't that they were trying to destroy the credibility of the government – I'm sure we would try to do that too if we were in the opposition. My quarrel was that they were doing it from the provincial point of view rather than from an alternative federal point of view.

We probably have the most decentralized federal system in the world. And because of that, because the country is so large, there is a very real danger of decentralizing too much. If we had a unitary state, like France or England, we probably could decentralize a great deal more, because there wouldn't be these rival sovereign powers called provinces, which day in and day out assert not only their powers and their rights, but also their achievements – which, nine times out of ten, are Ottawa's achievements done with Ottawa's money. I'm not blaming any particular government for taking credit as much as it can. But I am saying that there is a danger.

In politics, particularly in a federation, problems are not settled once and for all; negotiations never stop. But negotiations are not the same as concessions. I never objected to a new distribution of powers in order to improve or modernize the constitution. What I objected to was the unilateral character of so many provincial demands. The devolution of powers shouldn't only go in the direction of the provinces. If we want a strong and united Canada, there are certain powers – with respect to the economic union, for example – that should flow in the other direction.

241

I believe in federalism as a superior form of government; by definition, it is more pluralistic than monolithic and therefore respects diversity among people and groups. In general, freedom has a firmer foundation under federalism. In the past, I had sometimes sided with the provinces against the central government, sometimes with the central government against the provinces, whichever was the opposite of the way the political scales were tipping, creating dangerous imbalances.

242

The political thinking of the *nationalist* intelligentsia in Quebec – that is, the kind that thrives on slogans and clichés – has always regarded me as a hard-eyed centralizer, whereas in fact I led the only government since Confederation that has ever given the provinces legislative power that previously belonged to the federal Parliament, and while I was prime minister, public finances evolved steadily toward decentralization of revenues and expenditures.

243

The provinces as a whole had progressed enormously since the end of the Second World War. Once freed of the tutelage made necessary by a wartime economy, they had moved massively into those economic and social spheres of jurisdiction to which they had previously attached little importance. Furthermore, these rapid budgetary changes had been facilitated by successive federal governments through transfers of income tax points. It gave the provinces a painless way of tapping financial sources previously reserved for the federal government.

But the feast had only made the provinces hungrier. Having outstripped the federal government in budgetary resources, they began looking for ways to outstrip it in constitutional jurisdictions as well.

244

Canada, along with Switzerland, was already one of the two most decentralized countries on earth with respect to jurisdictions and public finances. However, the two countries being very different in size, Canada needed stronger bonds to hold the parts together. Furthermore, although the Swiss comprised four distinct *nationalities*, they had developed a common sense of belonging over many centuries and would speak without hesitation of "the Swiss nation." Canada, in contrast, had grown territorially as late as 1949, and its writers and politicians were still seeking a national identity. It was my feeling that the major decentralization being demanded by the provinces would endanger Canada's survival as a country, and I was determined to resist it.

XXIII

WHO SPEAKS FOR CANADA?

No nation is eternal. The glue that holds it together, the thing that makes nationhood, is the free will of a sovereign people to live together. The nation exists, not because it has been held together by force or enslaved, but because every part of the nation wants to belong to the whole for a host of social, economic, and historical reasons. Every citizen, every family, every group, every region must feel that the chances of fulfilling themselves to the utmost are greater within a united Canada.

National will, to my mind, is different from nationalism. *It's a sense of belonging, a sense of patriotism, a sense that being together is better than being apart. Sometimes, I'm afraid, the will to exist as a country is not very strong in Canada. There are all kinds of centrifugal forces – economic discontents, regional discontents, social discontents – which have caused the national will to weaken. It has to be strengthened. The first thing we should do is ask ourselves: Do we really want to sacrifice something of our provincialism in order that we be a country or do we want to take the easy road towards regionalism or egocentric personal gain? Is it going to be every man for himself or is it going to be every man for his country?*

In historical terms we are on the way to becoming one of the freest, one of the most prosperous democracies in the world. We are the inheritors of two of the main languages and cultures of Western civilization. We've built a tremendous country politically and we've expanded it geographically. We've brought in some of the most progressive social and political systems in the world. We're a pluralist society. But look around. Talk to the people. Read the media. Listen to the grumblings. Canadians aren't happy with their fate. And this, in spite of the success of our country.

Nobody is going to write anybody some sort of blank cheque on the future of Canada: here's the cheque, now go out and cash it and you'll get what you want out of this country. It doesn't work that way. We'll get it if we fight for it. We'll get it if, in future, Canadians are more skilled, more energetic, and more purposeful than the citizens of other countries.

Canada has often been called a mosaic, but I prefer the image of a tapestry, with its many threads and colours, its beautiful shapes, its intricate subtlety. If you go behind a tapestry, all you see is a mass of complicated knots. We have tied ourselves in knots, you might say. Too many Canadians only look at the tapestry of Canada that way. But if they would see it as others do, they would see what a beautiful, harmonious thing it really is.

177

245

There is a sense of quiet pride which lies deep within many Canadians, a feeling which permits us, as we contemplate the future of our country, to savour those qualities of self-reliance and tolerance, of moderation and bonhomie which are so abundant here. Notwithstanding all of this, the professional pessimists among us say that we are all doubts and visions and confusions; that we are a youth suffering from the difficulties of adolescence. Well, let them moan; it is the unimaginative and the frustrated who are always the first to despair about the attitudes of the young. Youth is hope and adventure and confidence. And so is Canada.

246

Canada seemed to me an ideal country for a policy of greater equality of opportunity. A young country, a rich country, a country of two languages, of ethnic and religious plurality, and of federative structure, Canada also possessed a political tradition that was neither entirely libertarian nor entirely socialist, but rested on an indispensable partnership between government and the private sector, and on direct action by the state to protect the weak from the strong, the disadvantaged from the well-heeled.

247

Canadians are not inhibited by pressures of manifest destiny. Our destiny is what we choose to make it. And if we surprise ourselves from time to time by our own accomplishments, so what? If we find that there is fun in being Canadian, why not?

248

Canadians continue to cherish the value system which has made them among the most fortunate of all the world's peoples. A system which embraces human relationships – tolerance, friendship, love, laughter, privacy; a system which pays heed to the beauty of our country and seeks to preserve the balance of nature; a system which accepts the inevitability of change but which at least consciously encourages only those changes which respect, rather than exploit, the human spirit; a system, in short, which regards individuals as the ultimate beneficiaries.

249

The character of Canada – Canada's ethic, if you wish – is not marked or identified by a sense of eighteenth-century territorial grandeur or nineteenth- or early-twentieth-century economic ferocity. Canada is known to its inhabitants and to others as a human place, a sanctuary of sanity in an increasingly troubled world. We need not search further for our identity. These traits of tolerance and courtesy and respect for our environment and for one another provide it. I suggest that a superior form of identity would be difficult to find.

250

Nobody ever said that living on half a continent with two official languages, composed of people who come from every corner of the earth, who have added themselves not only to the original French and English, but to the aboriginals who were here before us – nobody said it was easy; and that is why we say it takes more courage to stay in Canada and fight it out and look for equality in the defence of our rights than to withdraw within our regional walls and say we will be among ourselves.

251

This country and this constitution have allowed men to live in a state of freedom and prosperity which, though perhaps imperfect, has nevertheless rarely been matched in the world. And so I cannot help condemning as irresponsible those people who wish our nation to invest undetermined amounts of money, time, and energy in a constitutional adventure that they have been unable to define precisely but which would consist in more or less completely destroying Confederation to replace it with some vague form of sovereignty resulting in something like an independent Quebec, or associate states, or a "special status," or a Canadian common market, or a confederation of ten states, or some entirely different scheme that could be dreamt up on the spur of the moment, when chaos at all levels had already become inevitable.

252

The answer is NO to those who advocate separation rather than sharing, to those who advocate isolation rather than fellowship, to those who – basically –

advocate pride rather than love, because love involves coming together and meeting others halfway, and working with them to build a better world.

253

I do not doubt for one instant that they would be capable of making Quebec an independent country. But I have always believed that they have the stature to face a more difficult and nobler challenge – that of participating in the construction of a Canadian nation founded on democratic pluralism, institutional bilingualism, and the sense of sharing.

In the era of the global village, the very notion of sovereignty is becoming obsolete, and it is to protect what is left of it that large-scale amalgamations are being formed. But Canada already occupies half a continent. To weaken it by dividing it would be a historic blunder of infinite proportion. We must not rend the fabric of this still-young country, we must give it the chance to grow and to prosper.

254

The die is cast in Canada: there are two main ethnic and linguistic groups; each is too strong and too deeply rooted in the past, too firmly bound by a mother-culture, to be able to engulf the other. But if the two will collaborate at the hub of a truly pluralistic state, Canada could become the envied seat of a form of federalism that belongs to tomorrow's world. Better than the American melting-pot, Canada could offer an example to all those new Asian and African states who must discover how to govern their poly-ethnic populations with proper regard for justice and liberty. What better reason for cold-shouldering the lure of annexation to the United States? Canadian federalism is an experiment of major proportions; it could become a brilliant prototype for the moulding of tomorrow's civilization.

255

A country, after all, is not something you build as the pharaohs built the pyramids, and then leave stand-ing there to defy eternity. A country is something that is built every day out of certain basic shared values. And so it is in the hands of every Canadian to determine how well and wisely we shall build the country of the future.

256

Time, circumstances, and pure will cemented us together in a unique national enterprise, and that enterprise, by flying in the face of all expectations, of all experiences, of all conventional wisdom, that enterprise provides the world with a lesson in frater-nity. This extraordinary undertaking is so advanced now in the way of social justice and of prosperity, that to abandon it now would be to sin against the spirit, to sin against humanity.

257

My faith in Canada is, indeed, based on my faith in the people. Throughout my years in office, that faith proved justified over and over again, whenever the going was tough and the reforms we were trying to introduce were being opposed by the multinational corporations, by the provincial premiers, or by a superpower. I invariably found that if our cause was right, all we had to do to win was talk over the heads of our adversaries directly to the people of this land.

258

Who speaks for Canada? Our strength lies in our national will to live and work together as a people. Weaken that will, that spirit of community, and you weaken Canada. Weaken Canada, and you damage all the parts, no matter how rich some of those parts may be. My friends, you and I must stand up for Canada, and we must see that there is a national government that has the courage to do so as well.

MAJOR PUBLISHED SOURCES

WRITINGS BY PIERRE ELLIOTT TRUDEAU

Against the Current: Selected Writings, 1939–1996. Edited by Gérard Pelletier. Toronto: McClelland & Stewart, 1996.

Approaches to Politics. Translated by I.M. Owen. Toronto: Oxford University Press, 1970. (Collection of articles that originally appeared in the Quebec magazine *Vrai.*)

Federalism and the French Canadians. Toronto: Macmillan of Canada, 1968.

Lifting the Shadow of War. Edited by C. David Crenna. Edmonton: Hurtig, 1987.

Memoirs. Toronto: McClelland & Stewart, 1993.

Towards a Just Society: The Trudeau Years. Edited with Thomas S. Axworthy. Translated by Patricia Claxton. Toronto: Penguin Books Canada, 1992.

All other remarks, statements, speeches, and interviews were drawn from the Trudeau papers (access restricted) in the National Archives of Canada.

SOURCE NOTES

I. THE DOMAIN OF POLITICS

1. *Vrai*, 1958; *Approaches to Politics*, 26.
2. Ibid., 75.
3. Ibid., 25.

II. THE GIFT OF LIBERTY

4. Remarks, Liberal Party Dinner, Montreal, February 21, 1971.
5. *Federalism and the French Canadians*, xxi.
6. Ibid.
7. Remarks, Liberal Policy Conference, Ottawa, November 20, 1970.
8. Ibid.
9. Remarks, Liberal International Colloquium, Ottawa, April 29, 1974.
10. *Federalism and the French Canadians*, xxii.
11. Ibid., xxi–xxii.
12. *Vrai*, 1958; *Approaches to Politics*, 49–50.

III. THE BASIS OF AUTHORITY

13. *Federalism and the French Canadians*, xxii.

14. *Vrai*, 1958; *Approaches to Politics*, 34.
15. Ibid., 31.
16. Ibid., 27.
17. Ibid., 34.
18. Ibid., 32.
19. Ibid., 33.
20. Ibid., 35–36.
21. Ibid., 36.
22. Ibid., 36–37.
23. Ibid., 36.
24. Ibid.
25. Ibid., 37.

IV. THE JUST SOCIETY

26. *Vrai*, 1958; *Approaches to Politics*, 84.
27. *Towards a Just Society*, 401.
28. Ibid., 402.
29. *McGill Law Journal*, February 1962; *Against the Current*, 134.
30. Official Statement by the Prime Minister, "The Just Society," June 10, 1968.
31. Remarks, National Conference on the Law, Ottawa, February 1, 1972.

V. TOWARDS A JUST WORLD

32. *Memoirs*, 224.
33. Speech, Ralston Prize, Stanford University, Stanford, California, 1990; *Against the Current*, 337.
34. Remarks, Mansion House, London, England, March 13, 1975.
35. Remarks, University of Alberta, Edmonton, May 13, 1968; *Lifting the Shadow of War*, 9.

36. Speech, United Nations General Assembly Special Session on Disarmament, New York, May 26, 1978; *Lifting the Shadow of War*, 28.

37. Ibid.

38. Remarks, Mansion House, London, England, March 13, 1975.

39. Ibid.

40. Remarks, Duke University, Durham, North Carolina, May 12, 1974.

41. Ibid.

42. Ibid.

43. Remarks, Liberal Party Dinner, Vancouver, May 1, 1971.

44. Ibid.

45. Remarks, Duke University, Durham, North Carolina, May 12, 1974.

46. Remarks, Liberal Party Dinner, Vancouver, May 1, 1971.

47. Ibid.

48. Remarks, Duke University, Durham, North Carolina, May 12, 1974.

49. Remarks, Mansion House, London, England, March 13, 1975.

50. Ibid.

51. Remarks, Canadian Nuclear Association, Ottawa, June 17, 1975; *Lifting the Shadow of War*, 24.

VI. ON FREE ENTERPRISE

52. "A Liberal View of the Economy," Canadiana Conference, Toronto, April 2, 1976.

53. Ibid.

54. *McGill Law Journal*, February 1962; *Against the Current*, 132–3 (slight amendment).

55. Speech, Ralston Prize, Stanford University, Stanford, California, 1990; *Against the Current*, 334.
56. Remarks, Canadian Club, Ottawa, January 19, 1976.
57. Speech, Ralston Prize, Stanford University, Stanford, California, 1990; *Against the Current*, 335.
58. Ibid., 335–6.
59. Ibid., 336.
60. Remarks, Liberal Party Dinner, Vancouver, May 1, 1971.
61. Remarks, Duke University, Durham, North Carolina, May 12, 1974.
62. Ibid.
63. Ibid.
64. *McGill Law Journal*, February 1962; *Against the Current*, 138.
65. Ibid.
66. Ibid., 138–9.
67. Speech, Ralston Prize, Stanford University, Stanford, California, 1990; *Against the Current*, 338 (slightly edited).
68. Ibid., 338–9.

VII. THE ROLE OF THE STATE

69. *Vrai*, 1958; *Approaches to Politics*, 43–4.
70. Ibid., 44.
71. Remarks, Liberal International Colloquium, Ottawa, April 29, 1974.
72. "A Liberal View of the Economy," Canadiana Conference, Toronto, April 2, 1976.
73. "A Conversation with the Prime Minister," CTV, December 28, 1975.
74. Remarks, Liberal Party of Canada (Quebec), Montreal, October 19, 1979.

75. *Vrai*, 1958; *Approaches to Politics*, 48.

76. Ibid., 43.

77. Ibid.

78. "Quebec and the Constitutional Problem" (unpublished), 1965; *Federalism and the French Canadians*, 28–9.

79. Ibid., 29.

80. *Vrai*, 1958; *Approaches to Politics*, 44.

81. Ibid., 84–5.

82. Ibid., 85.

VIII. ON DEMOCRACY

83. Remarks, Liberal Policy Conference, Ottawa, November 20, 1970.

84. Remarks, Liberal International Colloquium, Ottawa, April 29, 1974.

85. Remarks, Liberal Policy Conference, Ottawa, November 20, 1970.

86. Remarks, Liberal International Colloquium, Ottawa, April 29, 1974.

87. *Vrai*, 1958; *Approaches to Politics*, 77.

88. Ibid.

89. Remarks, Liberal Policy Conference, Ottawa, November 20, 1970.

90. Remarks, National Conference on the Law, Ottawa, February 1, 1972.

91. *Vrai*, 1958; *Approaches to Politics*, 78.

92. Ibid., 85.

93. Ibid., 84.

94. Ibid., 86.

95. Ibid., 88.

96. Ibid., 87–8.

97. Ibid., 88–9.

98. "Some Obstacles to Democracy in Quebec," *Canadian Journal of Economics and Political Science*, Vol. XXIV, No. 3, August 1958; *Against the Current*, 91–2.

IX. ON PARTICIPATION

99. *Vrai*, 1958; *Approaches to Politics*, 78.
100. Ibid.
101. *Cité Libre*, October 1965; *Against the Current*, 25.
102. *Cité Libre*, June 1950; *Against the Current*, 27.
103. Remarks, Vancouver Liberal Association Dinner, August 8, 1969.
104. Ibid.
105. *Vrai*, 1958; *Approaches to Politics*, 89.
106. Remarks, Mount-Royal Liberal Association, Montreal, November 25, 1971.

X. THE ART OF GOVERNING

107. "A Liberal View of the Economy," Canadiana Conference, Toronto, April 2, 1976.
108. Remarks, Confederation Dinner, Toronto, November 19, 1979.
109. Remarks, Liberal International Congress, Ottawa, October 6, 1979.
110. "A Conversation with Prime Minister," CTV, December 28, 1975.
111. Remarks, Liberal International Colloquium, Ottawa, April 29, 1974.
112. Ibid.
113. Remarks, Liberal Conference, Harrison Hot Springs, B.C., November 21, 1969.

114. *Vrai*, 1958; *Approaches to Politics*, 50.

115. Ibid., 63–4.

116. Ibid., 64–5.

117. Ibid., 65.

118. Ibid., 64.

XI. ON HUMAN RIGHTS

119. *Vrai*, 1958; *Approaches to Politics*, 80–1.

120. *Towards a Just Society*, 407, 404 (edited).

121. Ibid., 407 (slight edit).

122. *Maclean's*, February. 8, 1964; *Against the Current*, 216 (tense change).

123. *Towards a Just Society*, 413–15 (edited).

124. Ibid., 407–8.

XII. ON COLLECTIVE RIGHTS

125. *Towards a Just Society*, 408 (slight amendment).

126. Ibid.

127. Ibid., 412.

128. Ibid., 409.

129. Ibid., 410.

130. Remarks, Vancouver Liberal Association Dinner, August 8, 1969.

131. Ibid.

132. *Maclean's*, September 28, 1992; *Against the Current*, 269–70.

XIII. THE STATE OF QUEBEC

133. *Vrai*, 1958; *Approaches to Politics*, 70 (tenses changed).

134. "Some Obstacles to Democracy in Quebec,"
     *Canadian Journal of Economics and Political
     Science*, Vol. XXIV, No. 3, August 1958; *Against the
     Current*, 85–6.
135. *Cité Libre*, March 1961; *Against the Current*,
     143–4.
136. Ibid., 144.
137. Ibid.
138. Ibid., 145 (slight edit).
139. *Cité Libre*, April 1962; *Against the Current*, 167
     (tenses changed).
140. "Federalism, Nationalism, and Reason," address,
     Canadian Political Science Association and
     Association of Canadian Law Teachers, June 1964;
     Against the Current, 202.
141. Ibid.
142. Ibid., 203.

XIV. ON NATIONALISM

143. Remarks, Liberal International Colloquium,
     Ottawa, April 29, 1974.
144. Ibid.
145. "Quebec and the Constitutional Problem" (unpub-
     lished), 1965; *Federalism and the French Canadians*,
     12.
146. "Federalism, Nationalism, and Reason," address,
     Canadian Political Science Association and
     Association of Canadian Law Teachers, June 1964;
     Against the Current, 189–90.
147. Ibid., 190.
148. Ibid.
149. *Cité Libre*, April 1962; *Against the Current*, 156.
150. Ibid., 157.